Without Prejudice

Copyright 2003, Element Limited Corp.

All rights reserved. No part of this book may be reproduced, or utilized in any form or by any means, electronic or mechanical, including photocopying, recording, or by any information storage or retrieval system, without permission in writing from the publisher.

Non-Fiction
ISBN 0-9729814-1-1
Library of Congress catalog card number: 2003095728
First edition
Subjects: Business; management; motivational; self-help.

Also by the author:
Practice Without Fear – A Physician's guide to asset protection and Liability reduction by Roger Murray M.D. and Toby Unwin M.B.A

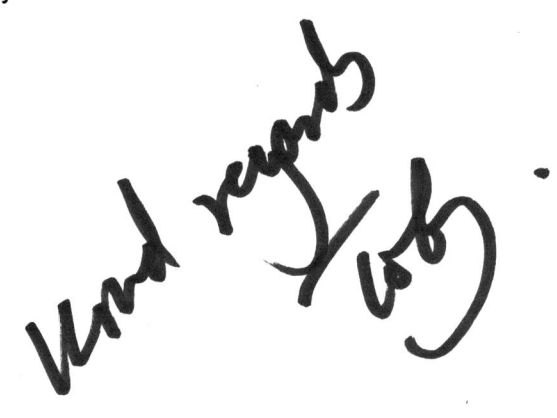

Legal Stuff

The rules in this book are my opinions, not those of the publisher, or any associated companies. Opinions may change, the rules here may not be relevant in your situation, or they could be complete rubbish; that is up to you to decide. You should make any serious decision after consulting competent professional help. Do not rely on this book to run your life; I cannot and will not be responsible for the consequences. While I'm on the subject: do not run with sharp objects; if you drop coffee in your lap, it may scold you; do not spit in the wind; objects in the rear view mirror are larger than they appear; and always look both ways before crossing the road.

Lastly, if you are easily offended, or think you might be a Flake, then I suggest that you do not buy this book. There are plenty of other titles that will not challenge the way you think, or suggest that you might not always be perfectly correct. Please do us all a favor and put this back on the shelf and look elsewhere; there are lots of books around with pretty pictures, you might enjoy one with a cloth cover, or that in which you can color in.

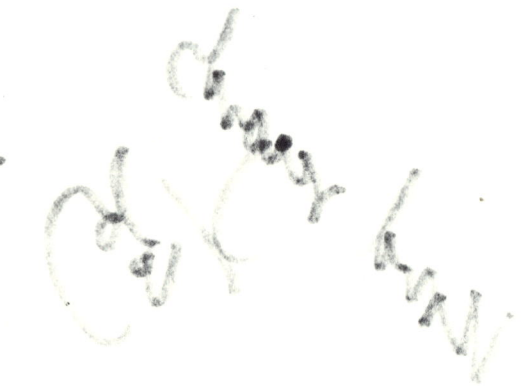

Acknowledgements

This part of any book is really tedious: you generally will not know who these people are and you do not know what they did. You will not know if you should be grateful to them for a masterpiece of literary engineering, or if you should be annoyed at them for wasting your time with such a piece of drivel. The bottom line: you do not *know* because you have not *read* the book yet.

Anyway, if you are really interested, we have put our "Acknowledgements" at the end of this book, so you can skip ahead to the back if you are bothered; otherwise, we are going to get started with the good stuff.

Contents

Introduction   5
    Why you need to avoid flakes.

1. What is a "Flake"?   8
    The unreliable people who waste your time
2. Their Background   13
    What have they done before?
3. Their Motivation and Character   40
    What drives them?
4. Their Actions   65
    What do they do, or not do?
5. Intuition   100
    Trust your gut.
6. What's Not Important   102
    Here are some things you shouldn't judge on.
7. How to Use the Flake Filter   109
    It's simple stuff.
8. How to deal with a flake   113
    Ok, you're lumbered, now what?
9. How not to be a flake   120
    Lift yourself above the crowd.

Extra Flake Filters forms   131

Copies of Flake Filter Certificates   138

Acknowledgements (again)   152

Introduction

The tools to him who has the ability to handle them
- French Proverb

We all rely on other people to help us in our projects. How many times have you been stuck waiting for someone else's input, for a document that you really need, for someone to return a phone call, or email, when you know they're not going to get around to it?

How much of your life has been wasted chasing people to simply do their jobs? How many times have people let you down by not doing what they said they were going to do? We're not talking about people trying and failing here, we're talking about people not even starting. Either they didn't think it was important, didn't know how or simply couldn't be bothered. The end result is that they didn't do what they said they were going to. Who suffers here? You.

Unfortunately this kind of thing happens every day. For example I need to find 1 builder to do some work to my house. I therefore have to make 36 calls. Why 36? If I call 36 guys only 18 will return my call. Of those only 6 will actually show up to look at the job and then only 3 will bother faxing in a quote. I need 3 quotes to ensure I'm getting a decent price, so I therefore have to call 36 people to get 1 builder!

Why is this? It's really simple. It's because most of these guys are flakes – they simply can't be relied upon to do what they say they're going to do. Incidentally this process is not enough to make sure they'll actually complete the job, it's the minimum you have to go through just to get someone who can start it.

We've all called customer service at some companies over a dozen times to fix a really simple issue. You get through to someone who really doesn't care if you live or die and they just want to get you off the phone as quickly as possible so you don't disrupt their life further. Whether they actually fix the problem or not is irrelevant to them – they won't have to deal with you the next time you call up. They probably won't even log your call – which puts you right back where you started from.

Not all flakes are as easy to spot as this, there's no central register of flakes you can look up. Many flakes have expensive M.B.A.s and doctorates. Many wear nice suits, drive great cars and work out of fancy offices. Some of them are outwardly "successful". Some talk a real good game. The difficult part here is that there's no singular attribute shared by all flakes, other than they'll end up wasting your time. Unfortunately that's something you'll only find out when it's too late.

What *The Flake Filter* enables you to do for the first time ever is to take all the little things and come to a conclusion as to whether or not the person you're talking to it going to waste your time or not. This can be really helpful for the borderline cases, or help you spot an area of potential weakness and decide if it's ok for you to proceed.

This is your cheat sheet to help you do the most difficult thing in business – assess people. It will save you time, and that will save you money. More importantly it will save your sanity, being able to find serious people who can deliver on their promises.

There are, however, some times when you can't help but deal with a flake. You may have no choice, they may work with someone else who is ok, they could work for the government, be a boss, or co-worker, or you can, quite simply, have made a mistake. The point is this is something that happens to all of us and you shouldn't have to put up with it.

You'll therefore be pleased to know that I've included a whole bunch of ways for you to deal with these people, to either cut them out of the picture entirely, or force them to get the work done that you need.

Lastly, I hope you realize that we're not perfect ourselves. We all have a bit of the flake in us, even me. I often assume, falsely, that people will do what they say they're going to do and therefore don't follow up. I set unrealistically short time frames to complete projects because I know that I can do the work in that time. If something isn't done I'll be up until 3AM doing it and sleep at my desk. Unfortunately other people you're relying on are not high performance individuals and can't be counted on to do the same thing. You rely on them, they let you down and therefore you wind up letting someone else down.

Enough. This type of crap has to stop. If I say I'm going to do something, I do it or fail at it. I don't mess around "strategizing" or saying I'm "too busy" (read can't be bothered). I just do it.

If you want to be a solid person and only deal with solid people then you need to read *The Flake Filter*...

1. What is a "Flake"?

The great question is not whether you have failed, but whether you are content with failure.
-- Chinese Proverb

Flaky people let you down. They talk to you about doing something and then do not deliver. They do not deliver because they are not capable, or because they lack the motivation to deliver. Unfortunately, the end result is still the same. We find the quote above interesting because it personifies Flakes – they fail to deliver, yet somehow seem not to mind this; to them it is acceptable. To you, as a solid businessperson, it should not be; neither should dealing with people like this be acceptable. Identifying these people has until recently been a hit or miss affair – "I knew he was a Flake because he let me down." Now you can stand a good chance of knowing before that can happen.

We operate from the premise that many people in the business world are in fact, Flakes. Scratch that. Most of them are, a few times a year you come across really serious people who deliver what they promise – they're worth their weight in gold. You may not always see it that way, but there is a reason "the world is so cruel," "you didn't win that deal, even though he gave you all the "*right* signs" and "the jerk didn't show up for your lunch meeting" – one word: Flakes. They are all around us and we must stop wasting away so much valuable time with them. *The Flake Filter* is our sure-fire tool against them, but first you must understand what it is we are fighting and how to do battle.

It is necessary that we first define a "Flake," so that you can easily understand whom you do not want to do business with and why. It will also be useful to understand who Flakes are, so you can stay far, far away from them and certainly bury any Flaky tendencies you may have developed over the years. We want to show you what a Flake *is* so we are all working from the same point of reference, especially since we are all on the *same* team against *them*. Then, we will show you how to instantly figure out if someone is likely to be a Flake, so you can move on to find some credible, quality person with which to do business with instead.

Our definition of a "Flake" is fairly simple: someone who does not deliver on their promises. This definition sounds simple, but as we all know, it is clearly not. There is no one factor that enables you to identify a "Flake;" it is a combination of factors, and they do not all score the same. This is why you need the filter to help identify them and run people through the same scoring mechanism each time, not a system that can change with your moods.

Flakes are usually unsuccessful business people (successful in the sense of fame and fortune – because it is the easiest and simplest definition most of us can agree on). Flakes usually B.S. around; they do not prefer straight talk, and they usually prefer small talk. They are full of it, and they try to convince you that they are not. Flakes sometimes believe there are economic systems out there better than capitalism. Flakes sometimes believe they are better than another person for various, unsubstantiated reasons (like class, wealth or education level).

Flakes are ultimately time wasters. Flakes are unreliable, usually lazy (which is why many bureaucrats are Flakes) and untalented people who wish they did not have to work, which is why they frequently try to take the "easy" roads, or just do not produce at all. You cannot learn any *positive* things from a Flake. You will not be able to do any *meaningful* business with a Flake. Bottom line: stay away from these people!

Now, to define the opposite of Flakes, we will explain what "non-Flakes" or "solid" people are. Non-Flakes are self-starters. Non-Flakes are usually entrepreneurs or business owners, or people who strive toward improving themselves. They are usually not bureaucrats or educators in the modern sense (educators in the traditional sense would be any person you learn important, meaningful things from that are applicable throughout life – most of us have only a select few teachers from our schooling years that fit this "traditional" definition).

The non-Flake is often a believer in life-long education, not necessarily academic learning, but all types of learning. Non-Flakes are competent individuals whom you can trust. These solid people say what they will do, and then go do it. Non-Flakes are quick with decisions because they respect your time and theirs; and because if something is a good decision, then there is no intelligible reason to drag feet. They admit mistakes, when they make them; and they learn from their own mistakes *and* the mistakes of others. There is a saying that states, "Only a fool learns from his own experience, but the wise person learns through the experiences of others." Non-Flakes try never to keep making the same mistakes over and over again.

People that are not Flakes do not necessarily have to be the Titans of Industry; they just need to strive to be the best. Even if you're a garbage man, be the best damn garbage man there is, no exceptions. These people usually strive toward being the top of their profession. Non-Flakes get satisfaction out of a job well done, no matter what that job is. Solid guys are usually competitive and will make sacrifices to win. Being a solid guy does not make you perfect, but being a Flake definitely makes you flawed.

Are you getting the picture about Flakes versus non-Flakes? We hope so. If not, stay with us a bit longer for it should all become crystal clear very soon.

Now, how do you "filter-them-out"? If you know what a Flake is and what a Flake is not, then how do you avoid the former and seek out the later? That is exactly what the *Flake Filter* provides you – the ability to sift or filter out the gems from the junk. It is really a simple process, which we will explain in great detail soon. For now though, you need to know that the *Flake Filter* is a scoring mechanism whereby Flaky people are identified for what they are, hopefully before they can do *you* much damage. Most of the time, you would be adding a positive two point score (for non-Flakes) or a negative two point score (for Flakes). If you are scoring yourself as a test, then give yourself an extra five points at the end of the test. Since you had the good sense to purchase this book and evaluate yourself honestly, you deserve something more for your reflections -- five extra points on the *Flake Filter*!

The rest of this book is mostly organized around explaining the individual questions to score in the *Flake Filter*. At the end of each chapter you will have the opportunity to fill in a scaled-down version of the complete *Flake Filter* for the section of it that was just covered. We encourage you to actively participate in these exercises as you read through the book so you gain a deeper understanding with instant applications.

By the way, this book is organized around deal making – what we believe to be the essence of business, and certainly capitalism. Many things on the *Flake Filter* refer to "deals."

This is not a mistake. We do not believe you have to be some Wall Street hotshot to be doing "deals." Doing a "deal" is doing business in our minds. Business always revolves around the act of selling or completing projects. If you are working in the business world, you are doing deals. These are the facts of the modern capitalistic system we live in, which by the way has swept the globe. If you do not like it . . . move to Russia, oops, move to East Germany, oops, move to Romania, oops, move to Cuba (at least until Fidel kicks it, then when all else fails, move to France). If you find that the word "deal" doesn't really apply to you then try substituting "project". We all have projects, things to do, and they're all a lot easier if we don't have to deal with flaky people.

This book is also organized around what we believe to be the way most of us meet new people and do business with them: after you shake hands and exchange pleasantries, usually you discuss each other's backgrounds (chapter two – history/past) to establish a foundation and credibility; then you probably discuss why they want to do this deal and how they will do it (chapter three – motivation and character) to build trust in their competence and game plan, as well as to make sure there is a strong motive for doing the deal; and finally, you see if they follow-through and actually do what they said they would (chapter four – actions). While this is a simplified system of how goods and services are sold or exchanged, we think it captures the essence of a transaction. Indications of Flakiness rear their ugly head throughout this process which enables us and now, *you*, to determine if you are trying to do business with a Flake or not.

2. Their Background

You can't build a reputation on what you are going to do.
- Henry Ford

There is much to learn from history and actively applying it. Flakes never learn from the past; they are just doomed to repeat it, as the saying goes. Non-Flakes always learn from history, personally and generally. With that in mind, the majority of the rest of this book is segmented into easy-to-refer-back-to sections that appear on the *Flake Filter* itself. Enjoy.

Have they done an impressive deal before?

This is one of the most important points on the *Flake Filter*. It is so important that it carries five times more weighting that most of the other points. The logic goes like this: if someone has done something impressive before, then they should be able to do it again, probably in half the time. In order to do the deal in the first place, they must have some resources, ability and drive to see it through. This is a strong indicator that they are solid people.

By "impressive," we mean "successful" in your profession. If you are a Laundromat owner, maybe "an impressive deal" means your acquisition of another store or of your competitor or just growing sales by twenty percent over last year. If you are a banker, maybe it means acquiring a profitable, long-term client. If you are an insurance broker, maybe your "impressive deal" is finally landing that last *Fortune 500* company in your territory that you have worked on for nearly a year. As you can see, depending on the profession, "impressive" can mean different and sometimes complicated things that can involve many moving parts.

By looking at history, we can help to predict the future. We somehow doubt that John D. Rockefeller and J.P.Morgan were Flakes. Their achievements were so great and numerous that the chance of their earlier success being a fluke is minimal. It is rare that people come from truly nowhere to achieve great things; even those from humble backgrounds usually have a record of achieving impressive things in their childhood and early life. Their later triumphs merely build on these.

When you read the biographies of great men (something I do often reading several books a week – ah, the luxury of retiring in your twenties, but we digress), you often notice things like sporting achievements, triumphs against adversities and disadvantageous social backgrounds. We are not saying that it is impossible to turn your life around and suddenly start a new pattern of achievement, in fact, quite the opposite. People point to men like Armand Hammer or Colonel Sanders as achieving success late in life, yet a careful reading of his biographies reveals a drive and involvement in business from early childhood.

As a bit of a disclaimer, throughout this book I use many examples of high-level success stories. I do not do this to be highbrow, it's because there are simply not many stories about the best mailman in Florida or a corporation's top janitor.

There are many success stories, however, about the movers and shakers of this world. We utilize these people's stories as examples as much because of their availability, as it is to showcase top-level people toward which we all should strive. Further, we use many financial related examples because that is the industry of which I've been a part and because far too many people are more ignorant than they should be about financial matters. It is our way to give you, the reader, applications of the *Flake Filter*, as well as useful insights about the financial world around us.

Anyway, having done an impressive deal before means it is likely they can do it again. Their ability to do what they say they can do is strong, and they are unlikely to be a Flake. You will be adding points to the Filter if they pass this question correctly.

Was it down to them or others?

One of the companies I was involved with gained a new investor, a good public company with a strong track record. One of their conditions in their term sheet was that one of their top financial guys would transfer over and monitor the investment. "Bonus," the board thought, "we know this guy has been involved in some great deals and comes from a great company; he'll be a real asset." A few weeks later it became pretty apparent that the guy was a total monkey. Every deal he eventually got into and touched turned to crap, and he was completely incompetent in handling even the most basic financial affairs.

When we were gearing up to sell one of our companies, this supposed "financial" guy was involved in doing the accounts for it. This guy prepared a balance sheet that we could not really understand -- his numbers practically looked like hieroglyphics. We initially assumed that this was because we might be slightly ignorant, since this "numbers" guy's financial knowledge presumably far surpassed ours. Later the auditors pointed out that the numbers were, in fact, completely rubbish and that we had been correct to suspect him all along. Basically, the guy was an idiot. The investors knew it and panned him off on another company -- if he had been any good the investors themselves would have kept him. Unfortunately people are often promoted way above their competence level.

A while later we ran into another guy, a legal one this time, who had done an "impressive" deal involving a large company going public. He went to great lengths to tell us that he had done pretty well financially by it, yet his financial situation did not seem to reflect that reality. This guy was far more interested in securing a large salary for himself than a decent equity slice, where the real money lay. We had a bad feeling about him, and we did not go into business with the guy which was a good call for us, because a while later we heard he had got himself into a large legal mess with one of the established players in the local business community.

We breathed a sigh of relief after we heard the gory details. Both of these guys were Flakes, yet at first glance and by conventional wisdom, most would consider them to be solid guys. What is wrong with that assessment? The simple answer was that they did not put the deals together. People with talent and foresight – people, who *worked for* these two Flakes, did the deals. These two Flakes were basically admin people in the truest sense of the word, and they had simply managed not to screw up enough to let their deals fail. They added nothing to the grander vision of the deals, nor did they work out any of the specific details of their deals. You have to dig deeply to uncover who the real dealmakers are in complex transactions.

The above examples form the basis for this next question on the *Flake Filter* – did they do the deal, or was it actually someone else. If it was down to them, kudos, if not then you need to knock some points off. Many people try to wrap themselves in the flags of successful businesses, telling you of their time at Microsoft, GE, First Such-N-Such Bank or a Big Five accounting firm. Ask yourself did they found these companies? Did they actually operate these firms at the highest levels? Were they personally responsible for tripling sales? Were they solely responsible for developing a world-renowned product? Did they do the underwriting and have complete signing authority? Did they orchestrate some monumental strategic alliance or acquisition? Are they personally responsible for branding the firm to the top of its market? Or, what is likely the case, did they simply punch a clock there for the last ten years?

Many people are in awe of certain companies around our world, and on the whole, we often agree that these organizations *are* in fact *quite* impressive. If you have ever worked at or with one, however, you quickly come to realize that superior talent is not necessarily spread evenly throughout the organizations – to do so would be nearly impossible for these multinational behemoths. Even if an HR department is as notoriously rigorous as Microsoft's, they will still get the occasional Flake that floats in through the cracks (probably, in part, because they did not have access to this book in the past). Understanding that most hiring departments are not nearly as rigorous as Microsoft's and assuming that skilled labor shortages continue, then you can imagine how many inferior "talents" are out there getting hired by desperate, top tier companies. It is one thing to have worked for a great company; it is entirely another thing to have been one of their top employees. Do not let the stars blind you to all the duds.

Basically, it comes down to the simply fact that if your guy did not do or was not involved *significantly* in the deal personally, then it just does not matter. The word "window-dressing" comes to mind. Add some points if they did the deal or were intricately involved themselves, otherwise subtract some if they did not, but are talking as though they did. You can embellish all you want, but you will not score highly on the *Flake Filter* if you are caught.

At what level do they talk and at what level was their last deal?

You know how it is, the guy is fresh out of business school, has never done any kind of significant business before (maybe he cleaned pools in the summertime or rented videos to you, but *let's be real*), yet he is suddenly talking about "seizing X%" of some business that Forrester Research says is worth $X billion. It's a load of wank (An English expression – *American* English translation: crap), and you know it.

A realtor I know talks about buying a $350,000 house to rent out. We know he is going to do it because he has a few of these, and this new one is not much more expensive than the others. I met a potential investor, and he commented on a deal he is going to do worth several hundred million dollars. He has done stacks of deals worth tens of millions of dollars and they seem to get bigger all the time, so we are inclined to believe that he will indeed pull this new one off as well.

I'm a firm believer in the "leapfrog" theory of advancing straight to the next level you want to play at. If a guy is plodding along with small deals, however, and is now suddenly talking about huge (one could say "pie-in-the-sky") plans while still pursuing the smaller stuff, you have got to be skeptical whether he will actually do it. I like "big picture" thinkers, but visionaries with no grounding in the details or experience in the smaller stuff that comes before the "big" deals, make me concerned.

One of my neighbors is the king of franchising. His average deal is about $10-20 million and he's been in business for 30 years. Every time I see him he tells me about new deals he's doing. He made $10M here, lost $60M a few years ago, but wasn't too bothered because he knew he'd make it back. How do I know he'll do what he says he's going to do? He's done this size of deal before. If he tells me he's putting $250K into a project, but expects it to be worth $15M next year then I'm inclined to believe him, because he does this stuff all the time and it's his level.

Now, he may not succeed at the project. The deal may not come off, but I know he'll give it a try. People see a successful person and assume that everything they touch turns to gold, it just isn't so. Every person has failures, the trick is not to make them too big and to keep back trying after.

> *"Our greatest glory is not in never failing, but in rising every time we fail"*
> *- Confucius*

The next time you hear about a deal that is being planned, ask yourself if it fits in with what the principals have done before. If it is totally out of left field then be suspicious. Many people we see with business plans claim that they are going to take the company public in two to three years, yet they have never taken a company public before, neither has anyone on their team, on their board, or anyone they know personally. This is the typically pie-in-the-sky, Flaky crap you hear every day, yet most people rarely challenge it. The next time you hear comments like, "we're gonna IPO it," and, "this will be an $X billion company in only a few years," think twice and question what people are telling you. Do everyone a big favor and do not take their Flaky comments at face value – punch a hole or two in their reasoning.

Anyway, when you are filling out the *Flake Filter* take two points off if the person is going completely from penny deals to dollar ones without passing quarter deals in between. If they have played at their current level before and are staying there (not trying to stretch too far), or have continually moved their deal size up all their lives; then add two points because odds are they are solid business citizens.

Do they have a track record in what they are doing?

This is a pretty obvious one to me, but many people will overlook it. Again, history is a *pretty good* predictor of the future (despite what the mutual fund prospectus is forced to say), but one's boldness (and others' blindness by it) will often overshadow this fact. While it is possible to succeed in some industries without any previous experience in them (in fact, sometimes it is even an advantage), it is rare to do so successfully and consistently.

Take, Virgin Atlantic Airways founder, Richard Branson as an example, one of my personal heroes and a totally stand up guy. All his life Richard has started new companies in areas he has known virtually nothing about. While he has taken a few knocks here and there, there is no doubting his outstanding business abilities and success. There are some sharp businessmen who can achieve success in a new industry without a track record, but we believe that they will score so highly on the other *Flake Filter* factors that we do not have a problem marking them down on this one in order to stay true to the *Filter*.

I met a venture capitalist in London that had just set up his fund. He was way sharper than the other monkeys in business suits that ran the majority of the old line, London VC firms. When we walked out of this guy's offices, we counted our fingers and expected a term sheet that would be rather onerous. We fully expected it to contain many pseudo-hidden clauses to gain control of the company we ran and provisions that would generally give us the shaft. The VC did not disappoint.

This fellow was a smart businessman and his fund had done pretty well as far as we know. His lack of actual VC experience did not hurt him, in fact, it probably actually helped him. This guy was, however, one of the exceptions that prove the rule. In general, if the person has a good record in what he is doing, then the odds are he can continue it. If he does not have any record in even a *similar* line of work, then you need to think twice about the likelihood of his (*and your*) success.

If someone can explain how their seemingly different track record is applicable in your instance (how it is transferable), and if their explanations truly make sense, yet just needed some "outside-the-box" thinking around it, then do not mark them down on this point. Just be careful about determining a "true" track record from a transferable one, since a solid guy will score so highly on the other criteria that this one will not matter much.

Note to reader: If you are standing in a bookshop still reading this, then go and buy it now. Do not be a deadbeat. Go to the register and part with some money. We are not giving you this information for free; plus you will need this book and these insights with you at *all* times to identify the various Flakes that pop up in your everyday life.

Do they refer to their business accomplishments, or instead mention previous employers and/or education?

I'm sure you have met them – "oh, he's an ex-Anderson guy," "I've eight years at KPMG," "she's a Stanford MBA," "when I was at Goldman Sachs . . .," "the five years I spent at Dell . . .," "Georgetown law wasn't nearly as difficult as I thought it would be," "I started at Cisco four years ago"

SO WHAT!!! I don't care *where* you worked before or *what* your education was. Some of the biggest Flakes I've *ever* met in my life are ex-Big Five guys, consultants or career *Fortune 500* employees. These people have a tendency to sit back and rely on the corporate name and aura to demonstrate a superiority they think that they have. Business books are full of far too many successful people that never even went to college, let alone a name school or worked for a name employer.

Some of the best businesspeople I have met worked their way through your basic state university or a second tier private college. Several other successful businesspeople we know went to work in their family's business or in a so-called "rough and tumble" businesses like used cars or selling timeshares, just to gain a certain level of experience to apply in other industries.

How many idiots have you met that says things like, "PwC recommended we do this with our car plant." Ask yourself how many cars did PricewaterhouseCoopers make last year? None! Yet, these people are perfectly willing to accept the computations of some trumped-up, sexy computer modeling program and their "solutions," over the experience, skills and instincts of the people *actually making* the cars.

People that lead with their previous employers or the schools they attended are some of the Flakiest, corporate losers I know. Ask yourself, "How does the fact that he went to Duke and worked at Bank of America affect you and your company?" It probably doesn't. Maybe that individual has some intellectual capital that is useful to your company (maybe not), but being a Dukie and an ex-banker should mean nothing, by itself, to you.

We are not saying that every consultant is a Flake. Clearly, there are some good ones out there. But, be careful because the top tier consultants try to wow you with their name, while the bottom tier, one man shows usually just try to take you *and* your money. Just working at a company whose main claim to fame is the amount of advertising it spends is not very impressive or even a guarantee of quality.

Certainly we noticed this with the amount of dot-bombs (err, dot-coms) that tried to buy market share without having a true plan for profitability. Yet, it did not stop many of the nation's supposedly "top" business school students from signing up at start-ups with visions of options and IPO's dancing in their heads. I'm all for entrepreneurialism but do not wear your dot-com company pink slips on your chest like they are some battle medals. If the company had a flawed business model, you should not have gone to work there in the first place just because your greed and the "greater fool" theory got the best of you. Next time, do your due diligence on the company for which you may go to work – they certainly do it on you.

There was this guy I used to work with that was introduced to us as being "ex Anderson." There was a long pause during which we think we were supposed to be impressed. This guy looked a bit Flaky in his purple shirt and was kind of effeminate. I thought this guy might be a Flake just based on those couple of things alone. Lo and behold, this guy was put in charge of Internet strategy for one of the companies in the group. We attended one of his meetings where the main topic of conversation was what was the right shade of purple for the website drop-down buttons. Inquires about how visitors would use the site or how it would make any money were quickly dismissed. Needless to say, with their reliance on and obvious infatuation with Flaky web consultants, that venture did not make it to profitability, or for that matter, sustainability – it is no longer with us.

We also have become rather cautious of "the MBA." Having an MBA does not, in and of itself, make you smart or brand you as a successful businessperson. I have one, but don't mention it unless someone asks. I know it really does not mean much in the wedge (English slang for money) making world. I'm reminded of the label from children's Halloween costumes, "Cape does not enable user to fly." An MBA degree does not make you a good businessperson. If you think it does, you are woefully mistaken. While it is nice to have, it is not the prime reason why you *might* become a business success.

"Most of these Harvard MBA types don't add up to dog shit; show me a guy that's poor, smart and hungry."
- Gordon Gekko, Wall Street

We are not, however, saying you wasted your money and time going to that prestigious school over the "just fine" business school program. A business degree can be a differentiator no matter what stage you walked across to receive it. But academic learning is very different from "real world" experience and the learning that comes with it. You can read and analyze all the case studies you want, but until you have actually put together a deal or won one, it does not mean much. As Mark Twain commented, "it is better to keep your mouth closed and let people think you are a fool, than to open it and remove all doubt." Do get a business degree if it helps you learn the "language" of business and allows you to learn from others, but do not dwell on your school's colors and expect to coast by on the mere mention of them. If you pretend, someone will find you out and you will have difficulty shaking the Flake moniker.

There is no escaping the *Flake Filter*.

Do they claim expertise they do not possess or cannot demonstrate?

If someone tells you they are an expert in something they are clearly not, or does not seem to be able to demonstrate this expertise, then they are likely to be a Flake. But how will you know if they are in fact, experts or can do the deal? Just ask them.

Ask them what deals they have done before and why the deal was good or what went wrong on the deal. Ask them what they learned from the deals gone bad and how they applied it the next time. Ask them how big the deal was and compare that to the industry norm. Ask them to explain the product or service and how many were sold, and so forth.

I have found that when you meet someone who is truly a master of their domain, their expertise tends to blow you away. They are *truly* masters of their universe. I recently opened an account with the private client group of a major bank in our area – the kind of people who only deal with accredited investors (basically, accredited investors have to be worth at least a million dollars or earn more than $200,000 a year for the last two consecutive years). But more important than the rarified air this puts you in, is the access this level of wealth brings.

The Securities and Exchange Commission (SEC) will not even allow advertisements of certain deals to non-accredited investors, *let alone* let them invest in these deals. These types of deals may be things like hedge funds or venture capital funds. These are some of the financial mechanisms that allow Mike the Millionaire to earn thirty percent or more in his hedge fund, while Joe Schmo plods along trying to find a certificate of deposit (CD) for four percent a year. That's right . . . you know these people; they call you excitedly when they can lock in 5.00% on a CD for sixty months. What they have really done is allow that banker to make probably double that return when he lends that money out. Getting back to our story . . . when I met this guy, after having met numerous other financial advisors over the years, I was "stepping into the light;" "when once I was blind, now I could see."

All the alternative investments I had been asking about for ages (usually falling on deaf ears) were laid out to me. New loan (leverage) programs were explained that were available only to accredited investors (substantially below Prime). Scenarios were discussed that could allow leveraging nearly every cent of my net worth with minimal risk.

This individual's mastery of his subject was all too apparent. He did not claim to know which stocks would go up, or which funds would go down. What he did *clearly know* was all the relevant asset classes and how they correlated to one another. He did not need to say he was an expert. He did not have to. His knowledge spoke for him. I would have given him the two points, while Fabrice the Flaky web consultant would have gotten minus two points.

Through your travels, you will, unfortunately, find many people with little or no knowledge in innovative technology and other cutting edge areas of business. Since it is so difficult to find knowledgeable staff, half-wits are often hired. Since most of the people these half-wits talk to *also* know very little, their incompetence goes undiscovered. This often becomes a vicious cycle – half-wits hiring morons who hire imbeciles and so on.

An example of this was when I sat in a meeting to brief a headhunter on the types of people we needed to hire for a company. After spelling out the need to find sharp, motivated, technically literate and presentable people for our company, I was staggered to hear another manager comment, "we want someone who likes a drink at lunch time and doesn't believe in working too hard." Amazingly, this fool was promoted soon after to be a senior director in charge of hiring for another company (a Flaky dot-com with some Flaky VC's money to burn). Be careful whom you work with.

How old are they? (Over 40 and unsuccessful is bad)

O.K., first of all this is not a chapter where I'm going to rag on old people and say that they are past it, quite the reverse. In my opinions, older people are very cool. They have been around for a long while, have probably made their fair share of mistakes and hopefully, have learned from them. Consequently, the really good ones have a level of experience you could not even hope to have. Older people also can view events from the unique, first-hand perspective of comparing them to other periods in history. Can you remember 1929 or the "nifty fifty" stocks of the 1960's "go-go" years? I can't, but I know some guys that can. They are sharp, and they recognized things like the dot-com craze as the hype and bubble they were. They have seen it all before, and it is rarely ever new news to them.

One of my closest friends is in his seventies. I talk to him everyday to gauge his opinions and get his advice. While I might not always follow it, I value it immensely because my friend is sharp *and* experienced. My grandfather, at nearly 100 years old, is also a very smart guy who has never used a computer, yet knows that the Internet and the Web is not the same thing. Most of the half-wits that do technical consulting do not even realize this.

Technical glossary point: The Internet is a whole computer "system;" it encompasses areas like email, file transfers, Internet relay chat, and, yes, the Web. However, the Web is only part of the 'Net and not the same thing. Incidentally, I still have an email address that is all numbers from the days on the Internet before there was even a "World Wide Web."

So, I imagine you are probably wondering where the title of this section came from. Let me paint a hypothetical (though all too real) picture. Say you have spent nearly three decades in the business world trying like hell to put together a winning business. You have probably had a few failures in that time, and hopefully you have learned from them. Remember, Winston Churchill defined success as, "the ability to go from one failure to another without losing enthusiasm." Somewhere along the line though, we hypothesize, something should have stuck, and you have "made it."

If it *did not* or it *has not*, then I believe there are only two explanations: either you are not learning from your mistakes, which in my opinion is a sin; or you have not tried hard enough – not made enough mistakes – and that, in and of itself, is even worse. I would rather go out there and screw up in a big way, than be one of those people who sit around saying, "*I* could do that," or "*I* should have done that," or "why didn't I *try* that." Much to the chagrin of people who have always told us that we are "burning the candle at both ends," it is better to aim high and miss, than aim low and hit.

I used to work with one of the founders of a very, large public company. This guy was a pretty nice person, and he had also been very successful. His company threw a huge party at a top London club to celebrate their tenth anniversary with the company's two hundred or so staff in attendance. I went up to him during the festivities and congratulated him on his success, saying that not many people could have done what he accomplished. This man was very touched and commented, "You're the only person here who's said that to me. I know most of the guys here sneer and say, 'I could have done that,' and they probably could have. But, the difference is that *I did*, and *they didn't*. They're happy to make their £50,000 (about $75,000) a year, but they never took a chance and so they're still stuck there now."

Examples like the above typify the failure to make mistakes. Most people are afraid of failure, when they should learn to embrace it. When you accept your mistakes and learn from them, then you have gained valuable experience with which you can use in other instances. Far too many people get *too* comfortable and complacent and then do not live out their lives to their fullest potential. Instead of asking, "what's the risk" if you do something different than the norm, perhaps you ought to ask, "What's the risk if I don't try something different?" Working so hard that you seem to be *trying* to fail, paradoxically, often leads to success.

Let us suppose that someone is over forty years of age and unsuccessful, does that make him a Flake? Not necessarily so. A Flake is someone who is unable to do what he says he can through a lack of commitment. If the guy is not promising to deliver the stars or do something else entirely impressive, but instead, merely competently delivers on his promises, then his age and level of success do not matter. If, however, an individual talks up a storm, he is older and he has still not made it, then it raises the question – what *has* he been doing all these years, and what is so different now?

Another slant to this issue is the level the guy deals at, which we dealt with earlier. I have met a lot of guys who are much more competent than other people, in essentially the same business, even though the later group of guys does bigger deals. The competent guys are usually in their fifties and still working on basically the same deal sizes that they did in their twenties. They are not necessarily Flakes; they just lacked the vision or the drive, and simply never made the move up. Should we deal with one of these guys? Sure, but only if it was at the level of deals they have always dealt in.

We would question their ability to suddenly move up if they finally tried after all those years.

I suggest you also be careful in how you apply this one, but do not ignore it, as it can be one of the clearest indications of ability. I recently came across a chart that gives one person's opinions of when someone is past their prime for their profession in the modern business world. The following gives some occupations/functions and lists the age at which someone should have achieved success, but is by no means inclusive, or the gospel. If someone is in one of the occupations below, hasn't "made it" and is past the prime age, then you ought to be leery.

Career	Age
Model	25
Athlete	35
Lawyer	35
Investment Banker	35
Salesperson	35
Management Consultant	40
Corporate Middle Manager	45
CEO	65

As people continue to live longer lives, the relevance of this question about their age will probably only apply to their first career. With people starting to seek out second and third careers, it may be more appropriate to ask, "Have they been in that high-demand profession for longer than fifteen or twenty years?"

There will always be careers better suited to younger people with more shear stamina for the long, erratic hours and constant travel. But, make sure a person on their second or third career was a success in their first (or has substantial reasons why they were not and how they learned from them), otherwise that person may simply be escaping their previous profession, and you may have another Flake on your hands. Also, there are many skill sets of younger-person jobs that can be applicable for older-person jobs. Many an investment banker or professional athlete have become successful businesspeople later in life by sharing with others the insights learned in their youth or the competitiveness learned on various ball fields. Going back to an earlier point: they may not have an *exact* track record, but they may have many *transferable* skills.

Applying the Background Criteria

On the following pages, we have an abbreviated version of the *Flake Filter* that covers only the background criteria we have just finished. Please take some time now to fill in the spaces with some of the people you know that may fit these criteria. Do not worry about offending anyone; no one needs to see *your* copy of this book. Just write in pencil if you have some aversion to writing in a book; it is *your* book after all.

All we ask is that you be brutally honest with yourself about some of the people you know and that you do not try *too hard* to over-analyze this exercise. If someone comes to mind for a particular question, then write them down immediately. If multiple people come to mind for that question and several other questions, be cognizant of the fact that you may be on to something . . .

Names:
1._____
   _____
2._____
   _____3._____
   _____
4._____
   _____
5._____
   _____

Have they done an impressive deal before?_____
_____
_____
_____
_____
_____

Was their "impressive deal" their doing or others?_____
_____
_____
_____
_____
_____
_____

At what level do they talk and at what level was their last deal?_____
_____
_____
_____

_____
_____
_____

Do they have a track record in what they're doing?_____
_____
_____
_____
_____
_____

Do they refer to their business accomplishments or instead mention previous employers or education?_____
_____
_____
_____
_____
_____

Do they claim expertise they do not possess or cannot demonstrate?_____
_____
_____
_____
_____
_____

How old are they?_____
_____
_____
_____
_____
_____
_____

3. Their Motivation and Character

Opportunity is missed by most people because it is dressed in overalls and looks like work.
-- Thomas Edison

A terrific professor in graduate school used to claim that what separates quality, destined-for-success people from everybody else was, "attitude, mentality and character." While I agree with this professor on these points (and think he was very astute on this point for an academic), I think one's motivation is also key.

Someone's attitude and mentality in life mostly affects their motivation and vice versa. Someone's character is also affected by attitude and mentality and vice versa, but it tends to be the core of who they are. Without quality character as a foundation, one's attitude, mentality and motivation will be poisoned in the long haul. But, then again, maybe this is paragraph is just an exercise in hair-splitting. Anyway, I believe the themes of this chapter do justice to this professor's philosophy about people.

Have you made money with them before?

This is the second one of the top three points that scores ten rather than two because it is *so* important. If you have made money with some people before, then unless it was a complete fluke, they are probably solid guys. As we stated earlier, most of the people you will meet in life are, unfortunately, Flakes. They simply could not put a deal together if they tried.

If you have made money with someone before, then they have presumably "walked the walk" and then delivered on something, at the very least. Every new business deal involves risk, but if you have already done well with them before, then it ought to suggest that they are solid, non-Flakes. There are a few guys I know that I have made hundreds of thousands of dollars with on various multi-million dollar deals. If any of them called right now, I would be on their new deal in a New York minute. These individuals have proven themselves to be solid. They do not mess about and, they are wedge-making machines.

Treasure these guys as you only meet a few of them in your life. No less an esteemed investor than Warren Buffet closed his first money managing operations and distributed all its capital only a few years into it. When he decided to reopen his partnership a few years later, nearly all of his original investors returned because they had established some history of making money with Warren previously. Had that not been the case, others and us might not be writing about him today. A history of profits is great, but a history *with* profits (for you) is always preferred.

It does not necessarily follow, however, that someone is a Flake just because you have not made money with him before. You may have just met them or the opportunity may not have been available until just recently. Remember though, if you consistently have not made money dealing with someone whose primarily role in your life has been to try to make returns on your money, then watch out and stick a negative two down in this box. Money Managers (stockbrokers, financial planners and so forth) are notorious for tripping on this last point. If you have been losing money with them for long periods of time, how long are you prepared to wait until they finally turn it around for you (and maybe *only* get lucky)? There is no magic time period for when you decide they are Flakes for having not made any money for you. But, when the opposite has occurred, and they have made you money, stick with them and listen attentively.

Notice, I did not say, "stay with them if you *like them as people*." If you want to deal with businesspeople solely on the basis of whether or not you "like them," it is fine, just do not expect to ever do business with me. While you may find me likable (and me, you), it is never a sole reason to do business together. It is important to take *any* emotions *totally* out of the picture when making your primarily business decisions. If you happen to find out, after the fact, that your kids go to school with their kids, play soccer together and you like Impressionist paintings too, great; but make your main decisions on the cold, hard facts alone -- have you (or anyone you know – next section) made money with them before?

I'm absolutely amazed by how many wealthy investors (usually institutional money) stand by their investment guys, through money losing incidents, time after time. There are numerous stories about some hotshot's fund crashing and burning and even landing him in jail, but his original investors stand by him when he launches his next vehicle after "taking some time off," because, "he's just *such* a visionary and ahead of his time; the authorities just don't know *what* to do with him." We are not necessarily sure if the fraudulent money manager is a Flake (probably is), but we are *damn sure* the idiotic investors are.

Never do a business deal based solely on emotions; do it only if it makes *you* more money.

Has anyone you know made money with them?

This is pretty similar to the point we just discussed. If they have made good money for someone you know (and you have *truly* verified this), then the odds are good they can do it for you too. You might like to think of this as a multiplier-type criterion. If you have *all* made money, he is a superstar. If *none* of you have, then you need to be careful. If the guy has made your friend money and done a good job, your friend will likely tell you about it or refer him to you. Some of the best people you may meet often come via this route. It is like they are being checked out a little bit each step of the way by a network of friends. If this individual does not do a good job for you, then you are naturally not going to recommend him on to your true friends after the fact.

The sad truth in business is that most projects don't work out and most deals don't get done. It's that mixture of right people, right time and the right plan coming together that creates a profit.

Whenever I hear of someone making good money for friends, I always try to meet the individual and find out more about the opportunity because as I've said all along: truly solid people are hard to find.

Do they have a financial motivation for dealing with you?

I do not run a charity. If I do work I expect to get paid. If I help someone else to make money with their business, and it involves more than a couple of minutes of my time then I had better be receiving a percentage of the proceeds. I'm a pure, unadulterated capitalists and proud of it (*BUY MORE COPIES* -- see, it just oozes from me. While we are on the topic, you will need to buy a copy for work, one for home and one for your car. This book will also make a great gift for Christmas, birthdays, weddings, anniversaries, christenings, bar mitzvah's, Kwanzaa celebrations, Ramadan and any other event you might schlep into Hallmark for). This is how our capitalistic system works -- the exchange of goods or services for payment, or other goods or services.

Yet, there are some people who do not seem to think in this way, even in America ("the promised land," as I call it). These types of people get involved in businesses for any number of reasons: fame; to feel important; because it sounds exciting, rewarding or prestigious; to help the community; to give themselves a sense of worth; to give themselves something to do; to meet the opposite sex; to play with cool "toys;" and so forth. In short, earning money to achieve financial independence *is not* their primary, motivating factor.

Now, this is all well and good when these people are off doing their own thing and not bothering anyone. If they are enjoying themselves, finding "meaning" and not getting in the way of our money creation activities, then good for them. Unfortunately every now and then, one of them will want to try and do a deal with you, and this is when this natural order of things can come unglued.

When I do deals, our motivation is quite simple: I want to make as much return on my money or time as possible, in as short a period of time as possible. I have no problem doing this and am quite open that this is why we are in the deal.

Nonetheless, it never ceases to amaze me the crazy ideas I hear and business plans I see. Take bars and restaurants for example. There are numerous people that want to own and operate one of these "businesses" (we only put quotations around the word because to call most of these enterprises "businesses," probably violates the unspoken rule number one of the business world: make a profit, don't lose money). Every decent businessperson knows that bars and restaurants are difficult to run and usually not profitable (if it becomes profitable, it is probably a franchise, a new fad that will eventually fade, or in the case of some ethnic restaurants a front for laundering money), and yet people long to own them.

The problem as I see it is that these people view the ownership of one of these establishments as an exciting, cool, good place to hang out with their friends, or worse, they think it will give them some type of prestige. Their emotions rule their decisions about this business, which probably violates rule number two in the business world: don't listen purely to your emotions. Money is often the last thing on their minds, and as a result, the business is a long-term (or short-term, depending on how fast they blow it), costly headache.

Unfortunately, people often bring these emotive notions into their business dealings with you. When someone asks me for a percentage of a deal, immediately I'm pleased because I know they will work their ass off to make it happen and make it highly profitable. Yet, it always gives me pangs of dread when I'm not asked, or worse have my offer of a percentage for doing the work, turned down.

In my numerous fund raising efforts, I have run into many people who have *offered* to help. Some claim to be doing it for the good of the community and do not want any money, even if they somehow find us some capital. With only a couple of notable exceptions, these are some of the biggest Flakes you will ever meet. The main reason they are complete Flakes is that it does not *really* affect them one way or the other if you get your deal done. They just want to be involved for personal reasons all of their own, and very often if they are not helping, then they are in the way.

Avoid these people like the plague. You will find them often in government, committees, not-for-profits, action groups and sadly, in education, corrupting another generation. They might claim to be on your side, and possibly are, but the bottom line is that they are nearly incapable of helping you, and you will spin your wheels trying to get something out of the relationship. Do yourself a favor and steer clear of these idiots. If someone is not motivated for financial reasons, be very, very suspicious.

Is their knowledge accurate?

It is truly amazing how many people really do not have a clue about their own jobs. A couple of years ago when we were trying to push a web site marketing product for one of our companies, we would ask marketing managers what their cost per visit was. They would usually stare at us blankly. When we would then explain that it was the amount they spent to get each visitor to their web site, we would get another puzzled expression. We would then patiently explain that they needed to take their marketing budget and divide it by their number of visitors to get this metric in order to start to try determining if their marketing was working and was cost-effective. When these marketing managers went through this exercise, they invariably found that the amount *spent* per visitor was usually more than they actually *earned* off the average visitor. We would then show them that by using our services, the cost per visit would be slashed and maybe, just maybe, they could even make a . . . profit!

For some reason though, we rarely got a sale, even though we would offer the following guarantee: if we don't get you X thousand visitors for our fee then it's free, just don't pay us. We were *that* confident of our firm's abilities. Still, we received no sales. We quickly realized after a little while that in order to make the sale, these marketing guys would basically have to admit that they did not know what the hell they were doing, had totally screwed up and everything they had previously done was probably wrong. They preferred to struggle on in their blindness and ordered another load of money losing banner ads. These people were total monkeys (no offense to those creatures), and they were Flakes too. Their lack of actually accurate knowledge demonstrated this plainly.

If someone does not know what they are doing when they are dealing with you, then there is only one way they can pass the *Flake Filter* on this point: admit they do not know and either back out of the way, bring themselves up to speed with the knowledge, or find someone who does know how to help. Admitting you do not know is not wrong or even a horrible thing. I believe it is a sign of strength. If you tell me you are weak in one area, but claim to be strong in another, then I'm inclined to believe you since you have already demonstrated your honesty and competence. In other words, admitting you do not know usually means you have the courage to not be a Flake.

> *"Paradoxically, when dumb money acknowledges its limitations, it ceases to be dumb."*
> *- Warren Buffet*

Now, I have two caveats. If you do not know something and admit this, yet this information is crucial to your task, I will be suspicious. Equally concerning, is if you do not know and admit this, yet show no desire to find out and learn, or show no initiative to find someone that does. In either of these situations, we will score you negative two points and be deeply suspicious of your character.

Have you caught them out in a lie?

This question is a tricky one. It is tricky because everyone lies. I lie. You lie. Everyone lies. And, you are a liar if you do not admit this. You need to lie, to some extent, just to get through life –
  "I had a really great time,
  "I like your new haircut"
  "No I don't mind doing that"
  "Everything's fine, what about you"
  "Of course you don't look fat"
  "Your casserole was excellent"
and so on. People lie *constantly!*

The shading of truths (lies) goes on all the time in the modern business world. "Truth Management" is a necessary skill. Some people even have to do it as part of their profession. When I was a headhunter, it was the industry standard to use a pseudonym to approach someone to offer them a job. You simply cannot phone up and say, "Hi, I'm a recruiter. Please can you tell me who your best project managers are so I can headhunt them?" No, some subterfuge is required (i.e. a lie).

There are also lies of omission all around us. Some guy is not going to tell you something detrimental about himself, even if it would have been important for you to know. I do not think you can really classify this type of "lie" as a true "lie" in the business world since everyone is constantly selling to each other (and you are really pretty dumb if you reel off a list of all the deals you screwed up or things you failed at). While everyone has these failures, most successful people are known for their achievements. If you somehow doubt this, then just look at the careers of people like Donald Trump, Larry Ellison, Rupert Murdoch, and others that have had roller coaster careers. All of these men have had some very serious down points in their careers, yet managed to recover from them. Today, none of these people are regarded as anything other than at the top of their professions. No, failure does not make you a Flake, giving in to it does.

So, if we can pretty much rule out lies of omission, then the next lie to tackle is exaggeration, or in the case of a negative incident, downplaying. Where do you draw the line? It is a tough one because these areas all have gray shades to them. These also become gray with time as people tend to look back on activities in their past from their own perspective and remember them from their own point of view – this is only natural as *they* were the ones there going through the experience. This is one of the reasons why we, as a culture, write down agreements. By writing them down, it avoids the, "I might have said this, but I meant that" routine.

I even bring this last point over to my personal life. When my wife and I have a major argument and reach an agreement after, we write it down. In doing so, we do not have to have that argument again because it is in black and white, and we have both signed it. Sometimes this does go against me, however, when I argue something and then my wife points out that I have agreed and signed something contradictory to my point. Of course, this pisses me off, but obviously I am stopped in my tracks because keeping my word is important to me.

When you run into people who say, "my word is my bond; we don't need to write anything down," be very careful. They may get indignant about you "not trusting them" and wanting an agreement, but what most sensible people realize, however, is that a written agreement protects *both* parties. When something is in writing it is easy to see who has erred.

Well, what about when someone lies to your face and you find out then or later that they lied? What kind of lie was that? Were they simply misinformed (no one is perfect or has perfect memory)? Were they voicing an opinion (everyone has one and many are usually wrong)? We do not think an opinion is a lie unless you stated it as a fact. The truth is, all of this is a very gray area and one you will have to use your own judgment on.

Is it a lie when it is really about something that is not worth bothering about? For instance, when telling someone the deli was out of pastrami simply because you forgot to pick it up? I do not think that is anything but a fairly minor lie. "I've been trying to get a hold of you," when you call, to which I usually answer, "well, you haven't tried very hard," is also fairly minor, but obviously easier to catch in these days of caller ID. Where you need to draw the line on lies is where it may cost you money.

One guy that called me was very pushy offering us a deal, despite our telling this person that we were not interested (this was the first warning sign). This individual told us of a supposedly great pre-IPO opportunity, but it had to be seized NOW (that was the second warning sign). We again told him that we were not interested, and then he said it was going to be a reverse-merger into a public shell, but he could not tell us the ticker symbol (the third warning sign). Finally, this guy said we could have our money back in a week after multiplying it ten times (those were warning sign numbers four and five).

The pattern of lies, that would have cost us money, made this Flake easy to spot. Despite the advent of the Internet seemingly making information so prevalent as to enable people to weed out schemers like this guy, it has had exactly the opposite, counter-intuitive effect. Schemes like the above seem to be growing like weeds because people cannot filter out all the information quickly enough to protect themselves (what a wonderful reason to give this book as a gift to the ones you love – sorry, shameless promotion).

The previous story's snake was a serious liar. Trusting him would have cost a lot of money, and that is where we draw the line. The other place we draw the line is when something is written down. Salesmen naturally exaggerate the benefits of their product, whether it is the latest widget or simply discussing themselves. We expect this. And it can be a little hard to separate the fact from the fiction, especially as the best lie is usually eighty percent truth.

When something is written down, however, it is a different matter entirely. Having something written down makes it easy to see if something is accurate and clear, and when someone has not delivered on one's promises. Incidentally, this is why many business development people in corporations have trouble getting their legal departments to agree to various brochure-ware pieces that they (the business development person) have created. Legal will tell them to say it, but do not write it down (unless, of course, they, the lawyers have sanitized it). In a court of law, nodding agreement or disagreement is the most difficult to prove, followed by the spoken word, and then the written word, which usually nails people.

The bottom line is this: you need to decide where you draw the lying line for yourself. If someone steps over *your* line, then mark them down on the Filter. If they have not crossed it, however, then give them the extra points.

Do they make a big show of their honesty ("The lady doth protest too much")?

The guy we discussed a few pages ago, who tried to sell a decidedly iffy load of stock, spent half an hour of his first conversation telling us how honest he was -- how he checked everyone out and dealt only with people of impeccable character. This guy claimed integrity was the number one issue to him.

"The lady doth protest too much."
- Shakespeare

Does the Pope bang on about being moral? No, his actions speak for themselves. Does Bill Gates need to tell you he is wealthy? No, it is pretty obvious if you have not been in a coma for the last decade. Does Arnold Schwarzeneger brag about how ripped and muscular he is, and that he could kick your ass round the block with both hands tied behind his back? He does not need to. Does Stephen Hawkins have to tell you that he is smarter than the average bear? No, again it is patently obvious.

Do you see where we are driving at here? These things are obvious. If you are the master at what you do, or you have special abilities that speak for themselves, then you do not need to talk up those abilities. I am probably not the best person to be pointing this out as I'm not noted for my modesty, but I have noticed that those that belabor these things are usually not the real deal. In fact, quite the opposite is usually the case.

When a person at some social function does not mention what he does, downplays it some or mentions it vaguely ("I invest in real estate and other things for a living"), then we dare say that *that* may be someone who is the real McCoy.

Dig in and question them to see for yourself, *if* they will divulge that is. Most of these types are perfectly content with themselves to lay low. They do not need to be showy, and they have nothing to prove.

In business, a certain level of honesty can be assumed. We should go with President Regan's treaty negotiation stance with the Russians, "trust, but verify." If, as the stock seller did, your guy lectures on and on about his honesty or tells you how very religious and what a good Christian he is, then be very wary. What's the worst-case scenario here? The guy could lose a couple of points here, but blow the rest of the Filter away with his solidity in other areas.

When someone claims to be a great Christian or extremely honest as a testament to how they conduct their business affairs, we should be first suspicious and then look to their actions (more on this in a later chapter). Best to err on the side of caution and mark him down if he slips up here.

Do they talk about having the resources to do a deal for 18 + months, but still have not done it?

We have come across many different people locally, a lot of whom have talked about setting up a venture capital fund, as I did and later failed at when I tried it again in the States. They said they were going to do it; they said they had access to tens of millions of dollars; and they also said they had access to all the best technology-related deals. When you bump into them a while later, they are at exactly the same stage in the process -- namely, the "just discussing it" stage or the "we're still putting it together" stage. The next time you see or hear about them, it has been many months later, still. What has happening to them? They boldly were going to do it, so why have they not?

The answer is probably one of two things: they lack one of the major components, in which case they are certainly Flakes; or they have the components, yet somehow have not got up off their asses to put them together, in which case they are also Flakes. If I say I am going to do something, it gets done. It is as simple as that. I might say I am thinking of doing something and not do it, or try and fail, but if I *talk* I always *do*. If you still have doubts about how many Flakes there are out there, then this simple point should get you thinking. How many people do you know that say they will do something, and then it *just never seems* to get done? If you are like us, then you undoubtedly know many, many Flakes that talk the proverbial talk but never walk the walk.

We have someone in town that announced the formation of a locally based venture capital firm. The local media jumped on this guy and made him an instant media darling. Suddenly, he was issuing press releases every couple minutes. He decides to do a fund; press release issued. He has some opinions on local issues; press release issued.

He has reorganized his desk; press release issued. He wets himself because of all of his press releases; press release issued. It was quite amusing indeed . . . now, perhaps we should not get entirely on his case. He was after all, just putting out announcements. Perhaps, we should really blame the lazy reporters who were spoon-fed their information and do not really want to *think* to write a story, but we digress . . . The interesting point here to note is that it has now been about six months since this guy was a flurry in the local media. His accomplishments to date are as follows: not even an offering memorandum (what you need to raise the money) to speak of. This guy's mouth was making promises, his actions have yet to deliver on.

This philosophy of not "walking the walk" became very apparent to me in the course of dealing with many of the lawyers I have met over the years. They all claimed the sun, moon and stars, and of course, their contacts would become ours once we were their clients. Since they *all* seemed to offer this *quid pro quo*, we comparison-shopped the law firms. Guess what? On closer examination, all these magical money contacts seemed to disappear, or worse, became one of the following: "well, I know this guy lives in town;" "have ya talked with this guy yet;" and "I golfed with someone who knows someone who used to date someone who might help you." It has now been years since we started having discussions with these Flakes, and still there is no progress from any of those local lawyers. Yet, these guys continue to make outrageous claims.

I have a friend who is trying to set up an Angel investor network, and naturally she went to see some of the same people we initially did. She told us the story of one, rather prominent local attorney who claimed (now get ready for *this* Whopper) that he would send wealthy people he knows, her way, "but when they come to you, they will not reveal that they are *in fact* my contacts; you will just have to know that they came to you to invest because *I* have secretly told them to and if you ask how they found you or why they came to you, you must understand that they will not tell you it was *me*, but you will know *it was me*."

Now, if you believe that line of crap, or for that matter crappy logic, then I have a very impressive sales development service you may be interested in. I will secretly develop business for you in return for twenty percent of the sales you receive. I also have several bridges in the Nevada desert to sell to you. As you can imagine, I have since decided to sit-it-out with many of these local lawyers. It seems fairly obvious now, they were complete and total Flakes.

A very practical twist to all this is the following turn of events, which we have seen firsthand several times. If anyone with a deal talks about having everything necessary to do the deal, and states that they are either going to do it, or are currently doing it, we should ask for how long these components have been in place. If the component parts have been in place for more that eighteen months and the thing still is not finished, then at best the people involved are idiots for not spotting the opportunity sooner, but more likely, they do not have what they claim to have.

People claiming to have two-thirds of everything needed for the deal, are a bit of a different matter. These are the guys who are more believable, and more likely to succeed. They know what they need, and typically are going after it. But, beware of the people who have been making the big claims for quite awhile, and mark them down on your chart accordingly.

Do they mention numbers in their discussions?

This is one of the most powerful points in the *Flake Filter*, despite being the last one mentioned in this section. It truly cuts through to the chase to who simply talks and who really knows their stuff and can do it. I once read a quote that stated something along the lines of, "if you are able to attach numbers to everything you do in your business, then you truly understand it and are a master of it." Many sales books tell you that you need to keep an accurate track of your calls and the types of calls you make -- whether they be cold calls, follow-up calls, account management calls, etc. -- so that you can accurately monitor your performance, be aware of any potential shortcomings and generally know what the hell you are doing.

The same lessons apply here in the *Flake Filter*. We met a guy once who claimed to have developed some graphical database engine, or something like that. This guy banged on about it for a while, claiming it was very successful. He supposedly had made a lot of money with it, yet he was very vague about how much or how successful (with some sort of metric) he had been. This guy did not really give us a good feeling, and we began to listen closer to what this guy was telling us; more importantly, to what he was *not*. This guy did not mention any customers, nor did he mention how much money he had made -- when someone is proud of their achievements, it is only natural to want to tell others about it. This guy did not mention any sales figures or product margins, in fact, most importantly; he did not mention a single number.

This guy was a major Flake. He talked many big plans, yet we were not convinced he would attempt them, let alone pull them off. So, we declined doing anything further with him. It turns out, in hindsight that was a good decision as we only hear talk from him, but never see any actions.

How did we avoid this business calamity that we might otherwise have fallen into? The numbers told us, or more appropriately, the lack of numbers told us. Numbers illuminate because they make things measurable. Numbers clarify, and they show us the way. Praise to the numbers, for they are our salvation.

On a totally different day, we went down to see a guy in Fort Lauderdale. He was an introduction from a business associate who recommended we should meet with him. The technology this guy had, turned out to be a way to slightly automate part of the gasoline delivery process for filling stations. This was not immediately exciting to me, and I mentally prepared myself to sleep through the presentation. When this guy started talking, however, something changed – it was the numbers. He knew all of them.

It turned out that his technology was only the enabler in a far bigger picture; he had planned a roll-up (consolidation of numerous businesses in one industry) in this staid industry. This guy knew all the relevant industry figures. He knew exactly how the number of gallons sold would affect his costs, his distribution, the number of staff he needed, his profit margin, his financing, and his bottom line. In summary, the guy was a genius, professional speaking, and we were very impressed.

It is totally possible that any other person could have given us the exact same pitch on the idea, and it would not have been nearly as effective. There are two main reasons why we say that: first, the guy had already started doing it and with his own money; and second, his grasp of the relevant numbers was so great that he did not need asking to tell us -

- every statement was backed up by a figure and he had an obvious mastery of how it all interrelated. This guy has gone public now. He told us he would when we met him, and he did shortly thereafter. Yet, every person we meet at some wine and cheese event tells us they are going to go public and does not, so why did we believe this guy – quite plainly, the numbers.

Anyway, back to the Filter. The next time you are trying to size up a guy, see if he is putting any verifiable numbers into his conversation. If he is not, then ask him some. Then, ask him some more. If he is evenly slightly evasive with any numbers, then you have got a Flake on your hands.

Applying the Motivation/Character criteria.

Names:
1._____
_____
2._____
_____**3.**_____
_____
4._____
_____
5._____
_____

Have you made money with them before?_____
_____
_____
_____
_____
_____
_____

Has anyone you know made money with them?_____
_____
_____
_____
_____
_____
_____

Do they have a financial motivation for dealing with you? _____
_____
_____
_____
_____
_____

Is their knowledge accurate? _____
_____
_____
_____
_____
_____

Have you caught them out in a lie? _____
_____
_____
_____
_____
_____

Do they make a big show of their honesty ("the lady doth protest too much")? _____
_____
_____
_____

Do they talk about having the resources to do a deal for 18 + months, but still have not done it?_____

_____
_____
_____
_____
_____

Do they mention numbers in their discussion?_____

_____
_____
_____
_____
_____

4. Their Actions

Actions lie louder than words.
-- Carolyn Wells

I chose the above quotation because it sums up how I feel about someone's actions. Their background, motivation and character can all be wonderful, but if they still do not show their competence in their actions, then they are probably Flakes after all. Actions speak louder than words is how the saying goes, but a "good" and slick Flake will sometimes stay undetected because actions can, in fact, lie louder than words. Let someone's actions speak for him, if they seem to do well on the first two parts of the Flake Filter. If this section of the *Flake Filter* checks out, then you are dealing with a genuine, solid businessperson, who is certainly not a Flake.

Do they deliver on their promises?

This is the third and final of the major indicators for the *Flake Filter*. It would also be the brightest spot on the *Flake Filter*, because the ability to deliver on your promises is ultimately what makes you a Flake or not. Why wait until a Flake lets you down on a big deal, when you can use this question to spot them easier?

- They swore they would send you a document, and they did not; mark them down negative ten points.
- They said they would arrange a meeting and did not; mark them down negative ten points.
- They said they would collaborate on a deal and then did not come through on their part; mark them down negative ten points.

People, who cannot deliver on their small promises, usually cannot deliver on the big ones either. It is an easily recognized pattern. Either their mouth writes checks their actions cannot cash, or they just lack the ability. Either way, stay away from these types of people. Not only are they Flakes, they have a tendency to piss you off too. Nothing seems to irritate people more than broken promises.

Those that *can deliver* usually do so on the small points too. It is a constant pattern with them also. After a few months of marriage, my wife decided that I was strange and different from other people – I did what I said I would. To me, this is basic. I do not often give my word, but when I do, I always keep it. A lot of people seem to have trouble saying, "no." They find that hard to do, but trust us, it is even harder to be a Flake – you have got to *work* at it.

We asked a high-net-worth guy we met to invest with us. He said no, to which we asked if he knew anyone who might be interested. He said he knew the right people, but he would not tell us. We asked who might be able to introduce us to the right people, and he gave us the same answer. Our wives thought this guy sounded like an asshole, but while we would have rather had the money or the introductions, we appreciated what he did *not* do for us – he did *not* waste our time or jerk us around. Because he did not promise what he would not deliver, we would be more inclined to do a deal with him in the future, as it is likely he would deliver if he claimed to.

There is a guy locally who works for a not-for-profit company whose *supposed* mission is to help the local high-tech industry. One of their main campaigning points is the lack of investment in the area, despite it being one of the nation's technology hot spots (how else to you think those theme park rides and space shuttles do all the wonderful things they do?). When we were talking about starting a company, he was extremely helpful and very supportive to us. He promised us that if we did this, he would be in our corner and help us all he could.

A few months went by while we prepared documents, but the moment we put our offering packet in his hands, his mood totally changed. He wrote us a bitchy email criticizing our statistics (which were directly quoted from some of his own reports), tried to bad-mouth us around town and generally made a nuisance of himself. We heard later he does this to anyone who tries to step on "his turf," and he has since succeeded in creating at least two factions in our region's technology industry – those few that support him and all others who do not.

Now, we both think this guy is a total dick -- that goes without saying – but, we also think he is a major Flake. Either he could not help us in the first place, in which case he should never have committed to, or he simply did not deliver on his promises to us. Anyway we slice it, he is a Flake.

Delivery on your promises is the main determinant of whether you are a Flake or not. Business is built on the back of trust, and trust depends on people keeping their promises. Essentially, that is it -- can I trust you to do what you say, or will you let me down and give me an excuse? If your guy delivers on his promises, then stick ten points down on this indicator.

Do they return phone calls and emails?

We are starting to get into a new section of the *Flake Filter* now. We have moved from someone's backgrounds and motivations, to their actions. Past history with someone gives you a good guide as to their ability and likelihood of doing a deal, but their actions are what will make the deal or "bring the deal off."

One of the first of these basic action indicators is, "do they return your first phone call or email?" There are a lot for reasons for not returning a telephone call or email. "Too busy," is the usual one you will hear. But let me suggest to you that very few people are "too busy" to make a one minute phone call or type for sixty seconds. What someone is really telling you is that you were not important enough for *them* to get back to *you*. They're telling you that they couldn't be bothered.

> *"Who is more busy than he who hath least to do?"*
> *- John Clarke*

Investment bankers and other financial professionals are famed for not returning calls. "We're so busy. Everyone is calling to get our money." These are the kind of excuses you can expect to hear from people in the industry. This is total B.S. though. If they cannot even have a secretary call you back to ask you to email a business plan or tell you not to bother now (because they are only investing in what the *Wall Street Journal* or *Red Herring* says is the hottest new technology this week), it is because they are not only rude, they are Flakes too.

It is quite humorous though to me, as these are the same guys who are always bitching about not getting any "good deals." There are probably a dozen "good deals" in their email boxes; they have just been too "busy" to open them. Or worse, they just deleted the messages; because someone they know well did not introduce the entrepreneur *directly* to them. Let's face it, lots of people are lazy and take the easiest and/or least confrontational route, even in the grand world of financing.

When we called a few existing funds and emailed a load of others, regarding investing with us, we rarely got a call returned. When we started to call some of the larger institutional fund investors, however, to talk about putting tens of millions of dollars with us, our calls were nearly always returned, even if it is just to say they are not interested. Intuitively, you would think the bigger fish would be "too busy," when experience shows it is exactly the opposite -- the smaller fish claim to be the busiest – perhaps their actions are why they're still small fish.

I've only ever met one guy in my life that I thought was "too busy". Ironically though, he was never too busy to get his job done. If he had to be there into the night returning calls he'd do it. I never once heard him say he was "too busy".

"None are so busy as the fool and the knave"
- John Dryden

Remember: the next time you are trying to get someone who is hiding behind voicemail or email, realize they are not busy, they are just Flaky. If someone cannot manage something as simple as a phone call, then what makes you think they could possibly help you in your project? Not returning your call is your first indication of Flakiness. Quality businesspeople will even return your message to say, "no thanks," rather than leave you hanging.

Have they engineered their own deals or been in the right place at the right time?

In every life the element of chance plays a certain part. Now, I'm not like those Flaky, mystical guys who believe everything is predetermined or that a higher power directs our every move. I firmly believe in the power of free will, otherwise what's the point to doing anything at all? I believe that man has the right and the ability to create his own destiny. All I am saying is that every now and again you get lucky.

I'm saying that luck is a determining factor. I happen to agree with the golfer, who when challenged on a "lucky" putt said, "You know, the more I practice the luckier I seem to get." I believe that you make your own luck, and as Machiavelli said, "build dams in advance, to prepare for the floods of misfortune." When I look at a business deal, I like to ask what Richard Branson does, "What's the worst that could happen?" And then, prepare for it. After that, I think what the best case could be, and *aim* for that.

Despite all this, even I acknowledge that "luck" sometimes seems to play a role. I happened to be in the recruitment industry years ago, and I also knew a little bit about the Internet despite working in a very successful, but technophobic firm, just as the online world was taking off. As they say, "in the land of the blind, the one eyed man is king."

This was the main success that has been the springboard for the rest of my careers. People will often look at someone and say, "Hey, you did that, maybe you can do this too." They will give someone the chance, but then it is up to that someone to perform. Without competent action on one's behalf, more chances would surely dry up.

I always knew, and firmly believed that I would ultimately be successful no matter what adversities were placed in my paths. My ex-girlfriend years ago, lost faith in me, and when she later discovered her mistake, my ship had already sailed. No doubt, my wife is grateful for this as she steps into her Mercedes in the morning and checks to see if she is running late on the new Cartier watch I bought her, but again, we digress . . .

A person I know is constantly taking credit for the deals his old acquaintances put together. This guy is like a leech sucking up as much kudos as he can for work he rarely ever accomplishes. His primary functions are the result of having been in "the right place at the right time" as well, but he epitomizes this lesson like no one else because of his ineptitude and stealing of credit for deals he did not engineer.

If a person seems to have a continual "lucky" streak, then the odds are, it is not luck; even if they make if look effortless (actually, *especially* if they make it look effortless). In the case of effortless "luck," it is *actual skill*, and you should acknowledge it as such, even if it makes you sick with jealousy to do so. If they have only had one good deal though, it is worth taking a look at it to see how it was put together. Maybe it was a fantastic deal at the beginning, that they became involved with, but they screwed it up so much, it ultimately became merely a good deal. Maybe their dad put it together, not them. Maybe there was some idiotic attorney who barely escaped killing the deal entirely, through some Herculean effort on the part of the entrepreneurs involved. Or maybe, just maybe, they were at the proverbial "right place at the right time." Whatever is the case, find out and if you do not think they were responsible for it, then mark them down accordingly.

Do they complete actions on time, or do they say they are "too busy?"

Again, this is a "delivery" item. Do they do what they say they will do, and do they do it on time? Being a Flake is a pattern that someone follows, just like being a competent person is a habit. Competent people are in the habit of delivering on their promises and completing actions on time. If you see them slipping on the small things, then the odds are they will slip on the big ones too.

When you call out someone on not delivering, and they say they are too busy, it is usually simply B.S. Were they *too busy* to go to lunch? Were they *too busy* to go out for a drink with their friends after work? Were they *too busy* to get up an hour earlier to tackle your project? No, they were not. They were just *too lazy,* or worse, they were just couldn't be bothered to do your stuff. They either did not intend to do it in the first place and lacked the balls to tell you no, or it is just simply not a priority for them, and they will get around to it sometime after they have untangled the phone cord and re-arranged their desktop ornaments.

The modern version of this "too busy" excuse that people hear a lot is the "they're traveling" line. Are they trekking by mule through some desert? No, they are probably flying from one city to another; they, of course in this day and age, have a mobile phone and a laptop computer, but it is mostly for show – they like to look *cool.* How many times have you seen people playing Solitaire on their laptop while flying at high altitudes? If they really took their computer to do work, do you think their boss would be happy to see them playing *that much* Solitaire on the job, during the day?

People today have no excuse for not getting a message and getting back in touch with you within a day or two, especially if they are just "traveling." If they are on vacation, then it is another issue entirely – they should have someone else covering or briefly doing their job for them while they are on vacation. If someone is just "traveling," at the very least, they should have assigned someone else in the office to deal with you or they should get back to you themselves within a day.

An airplane is a great place to work (unless you are flying it, which trust us, these guys usually are not). On a plane, you have lots of time to work with little to no distractions. You can deal judiciously with your emails and work on most offline documents.

Today, with the advent of email, you do not necessarily have to talk with someone to get something done. You do not even have to be in the same time zone. You can deal with a request at 2:00 a.m. if you need to, and the guy can pick it up whenever it is most convenient for him. "Too busy," or "he's traveling" are just <u>excuses from Flakes</u>.

Do not accept them.

Are you paying them by the hour, a retainer, or are they on a success-based arrangement?

As we saw earlier, if someone's financial goals are not aligned with your own, then the relationship is just not going to work out well. One of the ways to ensure that someone's goals *are*, in fact aligned with yours is to pay that person based on their performance. You pay a sales guy on his performance. You tip a waiter based on their performance. So, why should you not pay your lawyer, your accountant or your consultant this way?

One of the main reasons why most consultants are Flakes is that they are paid by the hour. I used to spend a lot of time with a guy who was a consultant. I liked him a lot, and we would talk for hours about a lot of different deals. The deals very rarely, if ever came through though, and we rarely did anything beyond *just talking* about doing a deal. As I grew older, I started to realize that the usual outcome of our meetings with this person was to set the agenda for another meeting, but rarely to actually *do anything*.

I mentioned this set of events to my father, who said, "of course he does that, that's what consultants do. If a project is finished, then they're out of a job and don't get paid anymore. They want to string things out for as long as they can." Sadly, this guy was used to this "consultant style," and he could not conduct business in any other way.

Now to pick on lawyers.

We generally despise most lawyers. We would rather go to see the dentist than the lawyer because it costs less, and you are better when you come out than when you go in – unlike at most law firms. Most lawyers are incompetent and greatly overcharge in my opinion. If we earned large hourly rates every time we did something related to our client's business, we would make sure we never finished a project either. This section got so large, I had to give it its own title:

11 Things lawyers do to waste your time and money – What you can do to stop them.

Charge by the hour
Most attorneys charge by the hour. That's good, right? You only pay for what you use? No, WRONG. They have every incentive in the world to drag out a project as long as possible and never complete it. If I offered to pay you $300 an hour for a project, but told you that when you were finished you would get no more money from me how long would *you* take to do it? It would never get finished, and there would be endless excuses as to why it wasn't and what further work needs to be done. Does this remind you of an attorney?

There is one lawyer I love though – my lawyer. He is not only smart and completely lacking in morals, he offers success-based rates. If he does not produce, then he does not get paid; it is as simple as that. Because he is not paid just for his time, any project gets done very quickly. Some people say, "don't you begrudge this guy the thousands of dollars you pay him for a few hours work?" Hell NO! I get what I want. I get it now, get it right and I do not get any rubbish about my lawyer having to "research" the subject on our time.

Ask how many hours the work is likely to take, multiply it by their rate to get their expected total cost. Now add 10-20% and offer them that as a flat fee. If they turn you down then they're planning to "run their clock" on you. If this is the case then get out of there and find a new lawyer quickly. You are best off offering them a small sum that should cover their costs, and then a large sum based upon a successful outcome. If the lawyer will go for this agreement then they're likely to get you a good result quickly.

If you can afford it put an attorney on retainer, you'll receive very quick service, done right the first time. If you have a successful corporation then for about $80K you can get an in-house attorney to handle all of your legal issues and you won't need to use expensive external lawyers.

Nitpicking
Attorneys are trained to find problems, and they're very good at this. Any attorney can find a problem in anything. Do not be naive enough to think that every legal contract is iron clad – it isn't. They'll bring this same problem finding approach to offering you advice. Ask them for a better solution, most of them won't be able to think of one, as they haven't been trained to find solutions. If the "solution" they come up with costs less than $100 of additional legal fees then go for it, otherwise they're probably just wasting your time.

It reminds me of a story about lawyers. A lawyer has had a client in litigation for over twenty years. He leaves his practice to his son to go on vacation. When he gets back, the boy says, "I did it, dad. I got them all in a room and we worked out their differences; the dispute is settled." The older lawyer grabs him by the ear and says, "you idiot, that case put you and your sisters through college."

It is said that in a town one lawyer can't make a living, but two can do just fine.

Legal opinions
The "Legal opinion" is closely related to nitpicking. When have you ever seen a letter from a law firm expressing an opinion that a planned action is 100% legal, no quibbles and they'd stake their reputation on it? Never. These letters are always C.Y.A. pieces of double talk and totally worthless, don't ask or pay for one. These guys will never commit themselves to anything, so this is pretty much useless information for anything other than to show to some half-wit who happens to be impressed by any document on fancy, legal letterhead.

Researching
What if you went to see a surgeon for a heart operation and he told you he'd have to research the subject first. You'd run, wouldn't you? What if he wanted to charge you for that? You'd laugh at him. If a lawyer is holding himself out to be an "expert" in the area and doesn't know something that's his problem, not yours.

"Researching the subject," by the way, is usually a total scam. Be careful not to fall for it. Most "legal research" consists of some paralegal making less than you do, photocopying law books you can find yourself in a library. Most legal documents can be downloaded for free from the Internet, and most legal forms that lawyers "have spent weeks drafting" are boilerplate documents they have their word processing department paste your name in.

There is a reason lawyer jokes permeate our culture, and it is not just because some are ambulance chasers; it is because they nearly all will sell their souls to bill more hours at *your* expense. Either ask him to recommend someone who does know, or tell him to look it up at his own expense.

Clock running
Most attorneys are paid by the hour. As we've already discussed, this drastically increases their incentive to find wasteful missions to run on your money, things are never simple and new problems always occur. When this starts be very firm and accuse him of "running his clock", he'll be indignant, then you can tell him that it's really very simple and XYZ other attorney offered to do it for a $500 flat fee – watch his attitude change.

The friendly chat
Your attorney is not your friend. I have a couple of attorneys that are my friends, but for the most part, when you're dealing with one in a professional situation he's just an hired hand there to perform an administrative function that would be totally unnecessary if we didn't live in a nanny state where lawyers write ever expanding rule books.

Now we've established the ground rules, don't engage in chit chat with an attorney, you'll be charged for this. I know people who don't even say "hello" or "goodbye", they just hang up the phone – it all adds up.

Boilerplate documents
These are one of the biggest scams that attorneys have going. Most people seem to think that contracts are written specifically for them, this just isn't true. They're printed off the computer and your name is substituted for someone else's. A friend was recently given a contract to read where his name alternated with that of the previous recipient. He had to make changes 4 times before the law firm got it right, and they gave him a $4,000 bill for it. Naturally the firm got that faxed back with a "to be discussed" appended.

You can easily download documents off the Internet that are near identical to those used by the law firms themselves. These documents vary slightly, so you might like to take them to an attorney to be "blessed" and printed out on their letterhead, but you will definitely save yourself all the expensive "drafting" fees they charge of booting up their word processor.

Business advice
Most lawyers don't know anything about business. If they were really knowledgeable they'd all be millionaires. They know next to nothing, yet seem to think they could teach Warren Buffet a thing or two. I fell for this, taking fund size advice from an "expert" attorney, and I've met a bunch of other people who got in a real serious mess by taking business advice from their attorneys.

I once got into an annoying loop of attending meetings with a CPA, who spent the whole time dishing up business advice to us. I don't have a high tolerance for this type of thing, so my comments quickly escalated from "perhaps you could give us some advice on XYZ instead" thru "We're not interested in stuff you read in the Financial Times and rehashed" to "Look, you obviously don't know what you're talking about here, can you either get on with this, or I'm going". Oddly enough we didn't receive an invoice.

Over billing
A prominent, young lawyer suffers a heart attack, only to awaken facing St. Peter at the pearly gates of Heaven. There had to be some mistake he thought, "I'm only thirty-five and too young to die.". "Young?" said St. Peter raising an eyebrow, "Why based on the number of hours you've billed to clients, you should be almost seventy!"

If the electric company over bills you then you're straight on the phone, most people are strangely silent when lawyers do it. Lawyers make mistakes too, and sometimes this kind of stuff is sadly routine, always check your bill.

Partner rates
You usually deal with a partner who "sells" you the services of the law firm. Many people think the same guy does all the work, that's just not true. Usually it's done by an associate, who then passes it on to a paralegal, who makes a fraction of this guy's salary and bill out at much less. However, when you get a bill, you are often charged as if the partner did the work. Ask him if he did, if he says yes then ask him a technical question about the documents, when he stumbles ask him to re-bill you at the paralegal rate.

"Non-negotiable" invoices
With all of the above factors creeping into an invoice, you will have a very strong negotiating position. Do not believe that just because it is on a law firm letterhead it is cast in stone. A friend of mine received a $50,000 invoice for legal work on a divorce that had not been completed. He said he was unhappy with the work, didn't have much money and was still not divorced. They lowered the bill to $7,000. He said he still wasn't happy, they said $4,000. "See ya!", he said, and they settled on $3,000 as he was walking out of the door.

Now not all lawyers are the scum of the earth. Some are actually decent human beings, and we'd like to thank them both for helping us prepare this report. As a C.Y.A. for us - always consult a lawyer on any legal matter you do not fully understand.

At the end of the day, it all comes down to whether the guy is going to be on your side or not. Does your success affect his? Do you both want the same thing? If you are not pulling on the same oar, then kick him out of the boat and stick two negative points on that *Flake Filter* box.

Do they talk in "MBA/consultant speak?"

"There's no visibility for the market," what the hell does that mean? I mean, we think we know. We believe it suggests that they do not know what is going on in the future, but we sure as hell would not bet the farm that *that* is what they mean. We are not even sure *they* know what they mean. But, damn, it sounds cool, does it not?

How about "bifurcate?" That is another favorite. Could they not just say, "Divide into two?" Fifty-cent words are great if you are trying to impress your teenager who is studying for the college entrance exams. I could certainly be using "bigger" words in this book, but in the spirit of being true to myself, I wanted to write like I speak. Not only can I reach more people if they do not have to sit with a dictionary by their bed as they read this, but I like to keep things simple as I stated before. If no less than Shakespeare said, "brevity is the soul of wit," then who am I to be overly wordy and complicated?

I sat in a wine bar in London and listened to this guy speak: "I want to disintermediate the consulting process . . . I want the customers to manage their own relationship . . . I want a knowledge base . . . I want to re-engineer the channels . . . I want to monitize the relationship, and I want you to help me."

He wanted *help*, but we did not have a clue *what* he was talking about. We wondered if *he knew* what he was talking about. I stayed quiet awhile and nodded wisely, and the guy carried on like this for over half an hour. After a little while later, it dawned on me, "Ah, you want us to make you a web site?"
"Yes, exactly," the guy said.

I wished that he had just told us that, rather than wasting my time with his drivel. The problem we find with "MBA/consultant speak" is that it can be used to describe just about anything, but you really cannot be sure of anything that is being said. It is much like "political double talk," but the purposes diverge. The purpose behind "MBA/consultant speak," is ironically to explain something, where the purpose behind "political double talk," is usually to cover it up or confuse. Actually, they both tend to succeed in confusing anyone who actually takes the time to listen to them.

I had an idea of a cartoon strip about an ex-consultant being laid-off from a Big Five firm, who finds himself continually down at the unemployment office. His employers keep finding out that he is a Flake, and they sack him. Each time he attempts to explain his "skill set" and "career methodologies" to some hopelessly incompetent government worker who attempts to find him a job for which he is suitable. Each time he gets a new job, he enthusiastically tells his friends at a dinner party or social gathering that he will be, "helping to re-engineer the customer portal," when he actually winds up cleaning the shop window; or "examining customer interface products," when he is actually having to pick up used toilet paper; "re-allocating client resources," when he is mucking out the monkey cage – you get the point. If any cartoonist would like to run with this idea, it can be yours for twenty percent of the proceeds. I would love to see it done.

Anyway, back to the "MBA/consultant speak . . .This language is purposely vague, and these guys use it as a crutch. It is like a lawyer falling back into legalese to explain a simple maneuver. He either wants to impress you, or he wants to cover up the fact that he does not really know what he is doing. We tell an entrepreneur that if they cannot describe what he does in plain English, than it probably is not a good idea. We want them to tell us about the idea in simple terms, take no more than a few sentences to do this, and whatever they do, do not show us a PowerPoint presentation.

I believe that these laptop run slideshows are an intellectual wheelchair. Sure, it is nice, bit-sized bits of information, but tell us a story about the product or service. Do not show us countless lists of bullet points, or worse, rely on a bunch of flashy animations to jazz up a very weak idea. Weave a creative yarn to sell us on your idea. Do you think Berkshire Hathaway needs to show one of these things to get investors to purchase their stock? No, we do not think so. An investor presentation does not have to be computerized with the same page layout and bullet point spacing we have seen a thousand times. **Do something original – tell us simply and in plain English.**

The only time you will ever hear me talking in "MBA/consultant speak is when I'm talking the piss out of someone, or when I'm trying to pitch an extremely weak idea to a half-wit (not that I do that often, mind you). My father, who knows a thing or two about consultants and their crap, told me recently to simply say, "I'm sorry, I don't understand what you're saying. I only speak English."

Waffle and verbal drivel is a sure sign of a Flake. It is also the sure sign of an entrepreneurial simpleton, who uses his language (and undoubtedly his degree) as a band-aid to cover up the gaping holes in his knowledge.

While we are on the subject and have a captive audience, we are also going to rag on "MBA books." I have read *a lot* of business books. I get through over a hundred in a year. The one type I avoid like the plague is the MBA/consultant type textbook, as I briefly mentioned at the beginning of this book. Basically, one of these academic/consultant guys will have an idea, often not a bad idea. It might be something like: do not bother trying to compete at where your industry is now; look at your company's strengths, examine where the future of your industry is heading and compete for that. There you go, the idea in one sentence. A paragraph is perhaps overkill. The whole back cover of the book, waffle. The acknowledgements, preface and chapters one through twenty-eight, all saying the same thing -- a complete waste of your time.

If you are an MBA/consultant type business book writer, do us all a favor and write up your idea in a magazine article instead. Please do not take up valuable shelf space with your drivel. Another cool trick these guys do that I have noticed is to list about twenty big companies and say that these firms are doing exactly what their book has recommended (usually the authors are doing a consulting project there). Hey presto, they have just guaranteed that all these guys will purchase a copy of their book for each of their employees and also send out bunches to their clients. They have just turned their pile of crap into an instant best seller.

Hang on, that actually is a pretty good idea…

O.K., the following companies are truly excellent and masters of the business domain. They alone represent all that is good in this World. They are the Truth, the Light, and the Inspiration for us all. They are the glue that binds the Earth together, without them we are nothing. They are the center of the Universe. They personify perfection. They are emperors amongst mere mortals, truly the wind beneath all our wings; the chosen few and kings of the wild frontier:

General Electric Company, Microsoft Corporation, Exxon Mobil Corporation, Citigroup Inc., Pfizer Inc, Wal-Mart Stores, Inc., AOL Time Warner Inc., American International Group, Inc., Intel Corporation, International Business Machines Corporation, BP p.l.c., GlaxoSmithKline plc, Verizon Communications Inc., Johnson & Johnson, SBC Communications Inc., Merck & Co., Inc., Toyota Motor Corporation, Cisco Systems, Inc., Vodafone Group PLC, Royal Dutch Petroleum Company, Coca-Cola Company, Home Depot, Inc., Oracle Corporation, HSBC Holdings plc, Bristol-Myers Squibb Company, Bank of America Corporation, Philip Morris Companies Inc., TOTAL FINA ELF S.A., Berkshire Hathaway, China Mobile (Hong Kong) Limited, Procter & Gamble Company, Nippon Telegraph and Telephone Corporation, Novartis AG, Fannie Mae, Eli Lilly and Company, AstraZeneca PLC, J.P. Morgan Chase & Co., Nokia Corporation, "Shell" Transport and Trading Company, p.l.c., Viacom Inc , Wells Fargo & Company, AT&T Corp., American Home Products Corporation, Abbott Laboratories, BellSouth Corporation, Dell Computer Corporation, PepsiCo, Inc., Allianz AG, Deutsche Telekom, Telecom Italia, Morgan Stanley Dean Witter & Co., ING Groep N.V., Aventis, Amgen Inc., Walt Disney Company, Unilever N.V., Medtronic, Inc., UBS AG, Chevron Corporation, Pharmacia

Corporation, Unilever PLC, Schering-Plough Corporation, Kraft Foods Inc., Sony Corporation, Texas Instruments Incorporated, Hewlett-Packard Company, American Express Company, Boeing Company, QUALCOMM Incorporated, DaimlerChrysler AG, Barclays PLC, AXA, Qwest Communications International Inc., Freddie Mac, Telefónica, Sun Microsystems, Inc., Ford Motor Company, E. I. du Pont de Nemours and Company, Taiwan Semiconductor Manufacturing Company Ltd., Eni S.p.A., EMC Corporation, British Telecommunications plc, Minnesota Mining and Manufacturing Company, Merrill Lynch & Co., France Telecom, Honda Motor Co., Ltd., E.ON AG, BANK ONE CORPORATION, Goldman Sachs Group, Inc., SAP Aktiengesellschaft, FleetBoston Financial Corporation, Anheuser-Busch Companies, Inc., Banco Bilbao Vizcaya Argentaria, S.A., Motorola, Inc., Mitsubishi Tokyo Financial Group, Inc., Enel S.p.A., Telefonaktiebolaget LM Ericsson.

If your guy insists on speaking to you in some trumped-up, yet childish language we call "MBA/consultant speak," then mark him down two points and do anything you can to get out of his presence.

Are they often quoted in the press, but never as having done anything?

There is a guy around here who works for a Big Five firm. I think he is a Flake, and I've never met him. Why should I judge someone so harshly that we do not even know? How could I possibly come to such a snap judgment, surely that is unfair, you protest?

I do not think so, and if you do not agree with me, I really do not care. I have got the money you paid for this book by now, and you will just look like a moocher if you try to take it back to the bookstore all dog-eared and dirty. Besides, as I explained before, this is a book about my opinions. If you want a book about your opinions, then please feel free to fill in the space at the back of the book – that is what it is there for.

Anyway, back to this Flaky guy . . . Just about every time I pick up the local business newspapers he is quoted in there. Now, if you think that most business stories are a result of investigative journalism, you are very wrong. As I alluded to earlier, what happens is that they receive a bunch of press releases that read like a story. The journalists, pick one they like (usually the least complex one to understand) and run with it. Sure, they may move a paragraph from the bottom of the press release to the middle of the story and other nifty tricks like that, but it is basically the press release with some cutting and pasting. If this media-whore has two or three stories in each paper I read (and I do not read them all), then he is probably sending out about ten press releases each week, at a minimum.

I think he does this because he likes to see his name in the press – some people are truly *that* narcissistic. He is usually quoted before his company's name and often his company is left out of the story entirely. If he spent this much time preparing press releases and then having to do the schmoozing and phone interviews that follow them with each journalist, it must take up most of his week. But the particularly bothersome thing is that he is never quoted as having done *anything*. It is just him giving his opinion on stuff, and as you know by now I could not care about someone else's opinion. Opinions are a dime a dozen; we want the facts.

There is another guy locally who does similar stuff also. This character is on a few committees also. All of this must take up so much of his time that he cannot have anything left for his day job. It comes as no surprise that on closer examination his projects have not moved forward one iota as far as we can tell. He is your classical triumph of style over substance, selling the sizzle without the steak, and every other metaphor you can think of for just being an out and out Flake.

But, there are some other people around here that you rarely hear about. They drop off the radar screen for months, and then appear in the newspaper having closed some impressive business deals. These are the guys we admire and it is them that we want to try to be like.

If you know a guy who loves the press more than the profits and if he sends out a press release every time he passes wind, then you have really got to question how much effort he will put into working with you to make some serious cash. Think about it and mark accordingly.

Are they punctual?

This seems a small point, but it also has wider ramifications. We do not like people that keep us waiting. I think it is completely rude, and as they say in the military, "five minutes early is on time." One of my many faults is being too early for meetings and having to spend ten to fifteen minutes kicking around waiting for people. I can get on with some work while I wait, or catch up on my reading, but being late is just rude and there is no excuse for it.

Being rude does not make you a Flake though. Punctuality is indicative of a couple of other things that relate directly to a person's ability to perform. First, if they said they would be there at a certain time and now they are not, then they did not deliver on their promise; it is as simple as that. If they cannot do something simple like be in a place when they said they would, then how can you trust them with a larger project? Second, if they are late it shows they cannot manage their time properly, and again, if they cannot do *that*, then they cannot be trusted to manage a project for you either.

This may sound petty, but Flakes are not immediately apparent to you at first glance. The whole point of this book is to allow you to put together a few small clues to help you decide whether someone is solid or not. The next time you meet someone, pay careful attention to their timekeeping, it is one of the first small clues you get to fill in the Flake Filter.

Do they like to talk "strategy?"

This is the second to last point on our Filter, and it is usually the MBA/consultant speaker who likes to do this. They are the types that like to talk "strategy." What this means is that they want to get together and talk about doing something, but not actually do it -- that would be reserved for another meeting; that is, if they get that far.

Successful people rarely talk "strategy," they just tell you what they are going to do, then go out and do it. They do not form a working committee. They do not research a focus group. They do not produce a thick report with a pretty PowerPoint show. They just do it. It is as simple as that. The furthest a couple of them might get down that "strategy" path is talking about which solution is best (there is little pre-solution discussion), then, once agreed, it is straight on to the action.

Those that talk "strategy" never get to the action. The actual action is not what excites them; they just like to *talk*, but not to *do*. Unfortunately, if you want to achieve anything in this world, you have to *do*. It is one of those inescapable facts, and nothing worthwhile is ever easy, even if you are a "top consultant."

People sometimes ask me why I became successful. I tell them it all comes down to one word, "focus." I make each project our one and only mission, and I do not stop until it is done. I do whatever it takes to achieve my goals. When I was younger, I was a Flake -- when things were hard or got boring, I simply gave up on them and started another project. Then one day I was faced with a set of challenges I could not walk away from. It was then that I found my focus, and the rest as they say, is history.

The thing that backs it up though, is that where others talk, we must do. This is often strange to most people. We ask them for their contribution on a project, and they tell us they were "only talking" about the project.

You can talk all you want, but it will not make you wealthy. You can try something and fail, and in my mind that makes you better than one of those guys who always talk, "what if" or say that they should have done this (yes, you *should have*, but you *didn't*).

Those people sit around and wonder about the roads not taken. I can tell you, I took all those roads, sometimes getting lost in the process and sometimes the car broke down. Other times, the road became some pot-holed piece of crap, but I took it anyway and learned from it. At the end of the day those that cannot *do* will talk, teach or consult.

Do not be one of them.

Applying the Actions Criteria.

Names:
1._____
_____
2._____
_____**3.**_____
_____
4._____
_____
5._____
_____

Do they deliver on their promises?_____
_____
_____
_____
_____
_____
_____

Do they return phone calls and emails?
_____
_____
_____
_____
_____
_____
_____

Have they engineered their own deals or been in the "right place at the right time?"

_____
_____
_____
_____
_____
_____

Do they complete actions on time or do they say they are "too busy?"

_____
_____
_____
_____
_____
_____
_____

Are you paying them by the hour, a retainer or are they on a success-based arrangement?

_____
_____
_____
_____
_____
_____
_____

Do they talk in "MBA/consultant speak?"

Are they often quoted in the press, but never as having done anything?

Are they punctual?

Do they like to talk "strategy?"

5. Intuition

He who has no opinion of his own, but depends upon the opinion and taste of others, is a slave.
- Freidrich Klopstock

Why do we have a section on "intuition" in a book called the *Flake Filter* – a method for filtering out people so as to deal with them strictly on fact, rather than on gut feeling? It is really quite simple. More often than not, when we have had a bad feeling about a guy, it has been borne out by our dealings with him or what we have heard about him later.

I do not believe that there is some magical, sixth sense that tells you these things. People have the capability to subconsciously put together small clues in their mind that are then assembled into a "feeling" about some situation or another. These "feelings" are then interpreted by many people as their "gut" feeling or "intuition." I don't claim to be particularly intuitive, indeed it is mainly seen as a female skill, one which, unfortunately, most men do not possess. But, on the few rare occasions I have had a bad "feeling" about someone, I have never been wrong.

I met with an investment banker who appeared at first glance to have an impressive background and be a sort of "can-do" guy. He would probably have scored an "OK", or maybe a "careful" on the *Flake Filter* based on the factual indicators, alone. Somehow though, I both got a bad feeling from the guy. I did not quite trust him, yet had no logical reason for doing so -- just lots of very small, possibly insignificant things led me toward that conclusion. I decided to give him a pass. There are lots of people to do business with, and I figured why waste time in a situation where I'm second-guessing my own decision.

If your guy does O.K. on the filter, but for some reason you do not feel right dealing with him, then don't. I don't claim that this thing is perfect, but it is very helpful and can point out areas of concern. At the end of the day, it is your call. You have to make the decision and deal with the consequences afterwards.

6. What's Not Important

Convincing yourself does not win an argument.
- Robert Half

I developed the *Flake Filter* to weed out the useless people that wasted our time. When I told people and friends whose judgments I value that I had this tool, they were excited. They wanted to see it too, for this could truly be "the Holy Grail of the business world" – the actual, very insightful comments of a friend of mine. Being the greedy capitalist exploiter that I am, I decided to write this book and maybe earn a little money from it -- as well as do my bit to highlight Flakes.

People gave some suggestions as to what they used to identify Flakes. Some of these were good ideas, and others did not make the filter. It might be useful to highlight which of these ideas were not a true indicator, and why.

Their level of spending – the kind of car they drive

I live in an upscale part of Florida. My neighbors all drive big SUV's, eat out at nice restaurants, have huge houses, boats, second homes, etc. – you would think they were all really wealthy and had tons of money. Sometimes, this just is not so. The car is leased. The meals are expensed. And, the houses are mortgaged to the hilt with their interest written off against their taxes. They often have little or a negative net worth when you add up all their debts.

You may think they are wealthy, but they are not. The average millionaire drives a three-year-old car, lives in a middle-of-the-road neighborhood and is rarely showy with his money. They spend less than they earn and have saved consistently over their lives, so now, they are rich.

Do not be impressed by the nice car and the platinum cards. They often have very little meaning. They are meant to impress you, but it does not mean these people are rich or any more competent than the next guy. Look at the man, not the Mercedes.

Their education or speech

A good education can certainly be an asset if you recognize its limitations. One of my best friends, a Yale graduate, told me that the head of his university says to each graduating class, "Congratulations, you now know nothing." Some parents are upset about spending so much money to have their children "know nothing." But, the wiser ones understand that a Yale education is like a pilot's license – a license to continue learning.

A breakdown of the richest men in the country, I saw, showed clearly that there was no correlation whatsoever between SAT scores, number of college degrees and wealth. After all, Bill Gates dropped out of Harvard and ironically, probably would not qualify to work for his own company according to their personnel guidelines.

The good ol' boy kicks the cow crap off his cowboy boots and asks, "how y'all are doin'," in his slow, southern drawl. A lot of people would think he is a dumb redneck, but then they probably would not know he owns a lot of the local, undeveloped real estate around here and is worth tens of millions of dollars. He is as sharp as a whip too – do not let the accent fool you. He could, right now, eat the lunch of any Ivy Leaguer speaking with marbles in their mouths.

A good accent often says that the bearer is well educated and from a good family. By contrast, a poor one often implies the opposite. However, it is my experience that for a guy with a distinctly working class accent to be cutting deals at high levels, he has got to be pretty damn sharp. I will count our fingers after dealing with that type of guy, to make sure he has not got one over on me without my noticing.

Their dress

I have wardrobes full of some very sharp, custom-made suits. I do not think it is an understatement to say that in a town where a strict dress code is no bare feet, I am frequently the smartest looking guy in the room. Back in London, a lot of guys have suits like mine. Unfortunately, like the Superman cape not enabling the user to fly, clothes do not necessarily make the man. Around here, a guy in a shabby pair of jeans will very often be more of a serious player than one in the Brooks Brothers suit. You just cannot really tell, so do not even bother.

The company they work for

Again, I think we have pretty much covered this earlier, but it is included again here because a lot of people use it as criteria when they should not. Some companies are very impressive -- they have excellent track records and have a great reputation. Companies are made up of people though, and, "a chain," as they say, "is only as strong as its weakest link." You need to evaluate each person you meet on their individual merits, not on how you view their company. An organization will often have lackluster people working for them simply because these are the gray men that do not stand out. Make sure you are judging the guy in front of you, not the corporate image.

People are often also impressed with titles. In the sales world a hefty title gives you instant credibility, so it is not uncommon to find dozens of "senior vice presidents" in a company. Banks are notorious for this. At many banks, the junior-level tellers are "assistant vice presidents."

Unfortunately, titles really do not mean much nowadays. Just when you start to believe it does, you will spot the puppet-master behind the executive puppet. I try to show the same amount of respect to people throughout an organization, no matter what their level or title implies.

Their offices

There is a set of Big Five firm offices in London I have spent a lot of time in. The lobbies are HUGE. The little space that is left over has offices in it, and they are scattered around parts of the edge of the building. The idea, I think, is to show people that not only are they a big, successful company dedicated to making money, but that they can afford to be silly with it too.

Opulence does not equal competence.

We have all heard about the guy who runs some hugely successful one-man show from a shabby closet office, his bedroom or his mobile phone in his truck. If your clients do not visit, then whom are you trying to impress?

I have visited some pretty impressive sets of buildings to chase up invoices. The companies usually look flush with cash, but in reality, they just do not have the dough. They are a couple of weeks away from going bust, and they are stringing out every invoice as long as they can. When someone's offices seem a little *too* nice, perhaps your instincts are correct.

One of the Internet companies I worked with, had offices in the centre of Mayfair, one of London's highest rent areas. "Why?" I asked. It was an Internet company -- it does not matter where it is based. It could be run out of some run-down building on the edge of town near some landfill. It was all a matter of ego – when it is unwarranted, be suspicious. Offices do not impress me, and they should not impress you either.

Are they a "professional"

We have discussed how people are overly and unnecessarily impressed by lawyers, accountants and other "professionals," earlier. Just remember that these people work for *you*. *You* call the shots. If they try to be too pushy or make you feel inferior to them, then walk. Just get out of there and find one who understands and appreciates who pays *their* bills. Remember, *you* are the one who employs them.

7. How to Use the Flake Filter

An executive is a man who decides; sometimes he decides right, but he always decides.
- John Henry Patterson

This thing is pretty easy to use. Even a Flake can use it. But, the whole purpose of these exercises is to be horrendously truthful. If you do not answer a question honestly, then we cannot guarantee an accurate evaluation or filtering. Most people want to be polite and give people the benefit of the doubt – now, is not that time. Rarely in any money-making venture should you "give someone the benefit of the doubt;" it will come back and bite you in your ass. Be calculating. Be hard and serious. Don't be emotional. "Just the facts ma'am," as they used to say in that old, police television series.

As we stated at the beginning, no one else needs to see your copy of this book – in fact, you should keep it with you as much as possible to practice these exercises. Think back to your school years: only when you practiced and did your homework, did you get good grades. It is the same with most things in life – do your homework, practice – in order to get good at it. You cannot expect to excel at something unless you work hard at it. With your wallet or your firm's pocket book at stake, you must be completely honest on your evaluations of the people you know or just met.

If your guy scores well on the criteria, then add two points (unless it is a shaded box, in which case you add ten points). If he fails it then take two points away. If you cannot make up our mind, then just add one. After you are done scoring him, add up your scores and compare it to the table at the bottom to see if he is a Flake or not.

Repeat this process as frequently as you can, because evaluating people is critical to truly great business success.

The Flake Filter

To eliminate those incapable of doing deals, or being unable to deliver on their promises.

Criteria	Score
Have they done an impressive deal before?	
Was it down to them, or others?	
What level do they talk at and what level was their last deal?	
Do they have a track record in what they're doing?	
Do they refer to their business accomplishments, or instead mention previous employers, or education?	
Do they claim expertise they do not possess, or cannot demonstrate?	
How old are they? (Over 40 and unsuccessful is bad)	
Have you made money with them before?	
Has anyone you know made money with them?	
Do they have a financial motivation for dealing with you?	
Is their knowledge accurate?	
Have you caught them out in a lie?	
Do they make a big show of their honesty? ("The lady doth protest too much")	
Do they talk about having the resources to do a deal for 18 months+, but still haven't done it?	
Do they mention numbers in their discussions?	
Do they deliver on their promises?	
Do they return phone calls?	
Have they engineered their own deals, or been in the right place at the right time?	
Do they complete actions on time? Do they say they're "too busy"	
Are you paying them by the hour, a retainer, or are they on a success-based arrangement?	
Do they talk in "MBA speak"?	
Are they often quoted in the press, but never as having done anything?	
Are they punctual?	
Do they like to talk "strategy"?	

Answers

-2	Bad
+2	Good
+1	Not applicable
+1	Lack of information
+10	Shaded box

Scoring

Score	Comment
Ticks in all the shaded boxes, or a score over 30	Solid guy
Score 20-30	OK guy
Score 10-20	Be careful
Score less than 10	Flake

8. How to deal with a flake

Either I will find a way or I will make one
- Sir Philip Sidney

We all get this eventually. Even if you apply The Flake Filter 100% accurately it can't help keep you free of all flakes. Eventually you have to deal with one, whether it's renewing your driving license, a project with a joint venture partner, or simply by making a mistake.

Just because you've got lumbered with dealing with a flake, someone who simply couldn't care if the deal gets done or not doesn't mean you can't do anything about it.

Try and get rid of them
Is it absolutely essential that you continue to deal with this person? If you've hired them then fire them. It isn't the people you fire that cause you problems, it's the people you don't. Ask to deal with someone else. Ask for their supervisor. Suggest you use a contractor to get the job done instead. Whatever you do, try not to deal with them.

Be firm
Most people are flaky because you allow them to be. If their not doing their job annoys you then tell them. People bully you because you allow them to. People look down their noses at you because you allow them to and people are flaky in their dealings with you because you allow them to be.

When you're chasing people up on the phone always take down their name, title and extension. They know you'll call them back if they don't do it and can maybe also get them in trouble with their bosses.

Put it in writing
I love contracts. They state very clearly, in black and white what is required of everyone. People's ideas and opinions change constantly – "I thought you meant that", etc.

Be very exacting as to what you specify in your agreements. Many of my neighbors have disappearing edge pools that "disappear" into their lawns. I wrote in the contract "a 6 foot tall man standing at point X on diagram 2 shall observe the edge of the pool to flow into the lake unobstructed, or pool is free". They had to re-do it 3 times to get it right, but it looks pretty good doesn't it?

Another good thing to do is to hold back the final payment until the contract has been satisfied. You'll find it near impossible to get someone to help you when you're no longer an active client.

Call them on non-performance
"You lied to me." Most people are very uncomfortable when you say this to them. They'll try to argue, to which you can say – "You didn't tell me the truth did you?" Follow this up immediately by telling them exactly what you want them to do to rectify the situation.

This is an excellent tactic as it puts them on the back foot and you in a very strong negotiating position.

Never get angry with flakes – if you lose control of yourself, you lose control of the situation. Calm, deliberate speech has a far stronger impact them a screaming, swearing maniac – anyone can do that when they lose their temper, you need to remain in control.

Do it for them
If you can possibly do it for them then do so. We've all heard the saying – "If you want something done, do it yourself". It's true.

Can you recommend someone to do that?
I often use – "Can you recommend someone competent who can do that?". The implication is that they're either not competent, or aren't going to do it. This puts them on the back foot of either proving they will do it, or shifting the task off onto someone else, which conveniently rids you of the flake.

Ask what are the stages involved?
The more you know about what needs to be done then the easier you can chase each person involved directly, or cut through the B.S. you're told about the task being "complicated" or "difficult".

When will you do it?
Ask them. Write it down. "So you're going to have this done by Wednesday?",… "And I have your word on that?". "Ok, I'll look forward to speaking with you on Wednesday at 8am".

Go over their heads
Last week I needed a document called a "verification of mortgage". A simple document nearly anyone in this company could have given me. Could have, if they were bothered, of course. I spoke to over 20 people in the company that afternoon before I got it. Why?

If they say they'll send it they won't. They'd lied a few times before and would, doubtless, do so again. The best way to deal with it? Call them on it – "Look, we both know you're not going to do it. Either fax it through to me right now, while we're both on the phone, or put me through to somebody competent".

When you're going over their heads don't settle for voicemail – "We both know they're not going to call back. Go and get them from their meeting to take this call… I don't care if they're meeting with the pope. Either do it, or find someone who can take care of this now."

Sometimes you'll hit an impasse. The person will claim they're the top guy, the boss is out, or just plain not put you through.

If they give you the boss is out excuse, ask for his mobile phone number. They won't give it to you. Say, I'll call him at home then and pause. They'll either ask if you have the number, or say they won't give it to you. Tell them you'll get the number off your private investigator for $30, it's just a small inconvenience for them not to give it to you. Here's the kicker – tell them that since you're a night owl you may be calling their boss rather late. Hopefully he won't mind, you'll be sure to mention them and say you're only calling because they refused to help... Now you'll get some service.

The other thing to do on hitting an impasse is to go online, search for the top officer and try the top down approach.

Chase them constantly
The squeaky wheel gets the grease. If there's a flake not returning your call that you won't have to deal with again afterwards then call them every 5 minutes. They'll get sick of it and do whatever it takes to get you out of their lives.

Tell everyone you're only waiting for...
This is useful for co-workers and those you need to remain on good terms with. If they feel people know they're holding up the project they'll work harder. If a few people ask them and pressure them too it's better than having to do it yourself.

The carrots
If you do this then I can arrange X, help you with Y or get you Z.

The sticks
If you don't do this then I'll do X, tell Y or take away Z.

"You're not going to let me down on this, are you?"
No one's going to say yes to this question. Now if they don't do it they've not only been flaky, they've broken "their word".

"I'm glad you're working on this as I know it will get done on time"
This is the flip side of the coin. You've built up an expectation and now they've got to live up to it.

Name drop
People who are well connected within a company, or industry tend to get better service. Subtly working a few mentions into a conversation with a foot dragger can work wonders.

Summary

- ✓ Try and get rid of them
- ✓ Be firm
- ✓ Put it in writing
- ✓ Call them on non-performance
- ✓ Do it for them
- ✓ Can you recommend someone to do that?
- ✓ Ask what are the stages involved?
- ✓ When will you do it?
- ✓ Go over their heads
- ✓ Chase them constantly
- ✓ Tell everyone you're only waiting for…
- ✓ The carrots
- ✓ The sticks
- ✓ "You're not going to let me down on this, are you?"
- ✓ "I'm glad you're working on this as I know it will get done on time"
- ✓ Name drop

9. How not to be a flake

Your determination will bring you much success.
- Fortune Cookie

Dress professionally
Most people make up their mind about you in the first few seconds of meeting you, before you even open your mouth. How do they do this? It's how you look, how you sit, how you dress. My father tells me he always looks at a man's shoes in an interview – if the guy doesn't take good care of his shoes, how's he going to take care of your business?

If you slouch, sit up straight. If you're overweight, go on a diet and do some exercise. Most importantly wear a suit. "It's not like that anymore", "we have casual Friday", I can hear you say. So what. If other people want to dress like slobs in front of clients that's their problem. When I'm working from home I'll go unshaven and answer my emails in my boxer shorts. When I'm seeing someone for a business meeting though I'll get out the Saville Row "Battledress for the board room" and polish up my hand made shoes.

I'll be the best dressed guy there and that puts everyone else at a disadvantage.

Get a good business card
Your business card is the first thing you hand to a new contact. In these days of "visit our web site for more information, we don't have brochures", it may be the only piece of paper you ever hand them, so make sure it's good.

As an aside, if you do send people to your web site then make sure it actually gives them information, rather than the usual "we are a pro-active, customer focused organization providing a wide range of consulting products and services to meet our client needs". This is consultant double speak and tells people precisely nothing about you, or what you do.

I have found that people still like to receive a brochure, even if they're buying an on-line product. They like to have something to hold and feel. A substantial brochure feels like a substantial firm.

Make sure your card is clear, not cluttered. Use heavy, textured card with raised type. Make sure it *feels* substantial. Most people won't read things you give them, but they will all *feel* them, so make sure they feel good. My attorney puts over 20 numbers on his cards and is equally uncontactable on all of them. Truly wealthy people have one number, an office where an assistant can place a call to wherever they are in the World. If someone has to guess which number to call you on, or you have to replace your business cards once a quarter because you've changed a number then you've got a problem.

Read what you write before you send it
This is something I fail to do, often. I think that just because I've written something it's therefore ok. It's not, your mind wanders, you make typos, etc. Read something aloud before you send it. If it's really important have a couple of other people read it as it can be very difficult to spot errors in your own work – as anyone who has a 1st edition of *Practice Without Fear* can tell you.

Put agreements in writing
This is very important. How are you going to stick to an agreement if you've forgotten it? How are you going to decide on a "grey area" if there's nothing written down to indicate what the decision should be? How can you hold

someone to an agreement if they can say "That's not what I understood."?

Everything must go in writing, from multi-national deals to your agreement with the lawn guy.

Here's a neat trick to bind someone to a contract even if they haven't signed it – Give them a cheque(American spelling – Check) with your terms written on it(either in the comments field, or on the back). When they cash it you've got yourself a contract that you can bind them to. Why?
- Offer – Your terms
- Acceptance – Their cashing it
- Consideration – The money

These three points constitute a legally binding contract. I've used "funny checks" to add terms into "unalterable" contracts with builders and also in dealing with my homeowners association – "Payment for all fines past and future". These guys have taken 3 such checks off me and they still keep cashing them!

Get a contact management program
When you're dealing with thousands of people over your lifetime it's hard to keep track of what you last talked to them about, what you promised to do, or when you should follow up next. If someone tells you to follow up when their budget's being put together in 4 months are you going to remember? If someone you've just spoken to asks you to call them when they're back from holiday are you going to remember that? Of course you're not. That's why you need a contact management program to stay organized.

Follow up
This is one of my weak points. I assume that just because someone says they're going to do something that they will.

More often they won't. That's why I make it a point now to mark in my PDA when to chase them up on it. I'll keep chasing them and moving the date forward until it's done. If you don't follow up, odds are it won't happen.

Get a PDA and keep organized
I have several thousand people's details in my Personal Digital Assistant(PDA). Now most of these people are losers that I only met once and won't be speaking to again. Occasionally though you get asked for a recommendation, have a need of their services or want to follow up on something. You can't go leafing through scraps of paper to find the information you need.

Keep every business card in a folder. Transfer anyone who may be useful into your computer.

Say no
It's a short, simple word, but most people can't say it. "Would you mind driving 5 hours to pick me up at the airport?", "Uh... ok" you reply. They put you on the spot and now you regret it. Here's what to say next time – "No."

You don't have to be rude, you don't have to raise your voice. Simply tell them it's not convenient, or you don't want to do it. You've saved yourself time, you've saved yourself resenting that person for the imposition and, more importantly you're probably going to end up letting the person down if you didn't intend to do it in the first place. Just say no.

Don't over promise
This is something most sales people are guilty of. Anyone can make a sale by lying about the product, the price, or the

terms. The best sales people are the ones that can ask for an order next time and get it.

I get several people to quote on a project. When I ask for a feature and a salesman shows me something can't be done, even though he knows it may lose him the sale it tells me 2 things. Firstly, it tells me that he's honest. Secondly, it tells me that the other guys who promised me the feature were lying and therefore can't be trusted.

If you over promise you can never deliver. You'll be a flake.

Deliver on your promises
This is the whole point of being a solid person. You must deliver on your promises. If you can't then keep your mouth shut.

Apologize early and often
If you can't deliver then let the people you are dealing with know as soon as possible and apologize, even if it wasn't your fault. They may be upset with you, but they will be much more upset if you waste more of their time, and will shortly come to be grateful for your honesty.

Give realistic quotes
If you know you can't do something, or that it will be a stretch, then don't promise you will – it sets you up for failure.

Quote in ranges
"How much will this cost to get fixed?", [sound of air being sucked though teeth], "Tricky, I really couldn't tell you, difficult job, see?".

Guess who's not getting the contract? Now I know you can't always tell people how much a project will cost down to the penny, but they can't make a purchasing decision without knowing if they're in the ball park. Just say something like "Between 2 and 4 hundred dollars, I'll be able to tell you more precisely after we start." There, that wasn't hard was it?

I have no idea how much it costs to fix plumbing, I'm not a plumber. It could be $40, it could be $40,000. I'll be getting 3 quotes, so I know I'm not going to overpay, but I need a price to see if it's in the right area. Your customers don't know your area and if you won't give them a price, or even an idea of it then you're wasting their time.

Admit when you're relying on someone else
This is something I'm sometimes guilty of. I tell people I'll have something done by Thursday, but I'm relying on someone else. They let me down and I end up looking like a flake. It would have been better to say "I can have it done by Thursday providing Stan comes though on his end."

Address your weaknesses
No one's perfect. We all have areas of strength and weakness. One of mine is chasing people to pay their invoices. I'm either too soft and don't get paid, or I'm so hard I end up ruining any business relationship I had with the client. I know this so I try to have other people chase my invoices, get paid up front, impose onerous terms for non-payment, generous terms for prompt payment, or use the client's services to offset against fees.

Recognize your weaknesses and address them. In business you can't be weak in one area, it will kill you. You can do everything else well, but if you can't sell, collect bills or take care of your accounts then your business will collapse.

Set goals
We all hear this so many times, it's barely worth repeating here. "Fail to plan, plan to fail" – we all know this. I thought for many years I didn't need to write my goals down as I knew what I wanted. Then I read that 80% of all millionaires did this. I was a millionaire, why didn't I? I gave it a go, just to see...

The results were amazing. Just writing the list clarified everything in my mind. I reviewed it twice a day and found myself ticking off achievements once a month. It was like the adult version of Santa Claus' wish list. You write it, it comes true. Try it. Just humor me...

Make to do lists
This is the follow up to your goal list. What are you going to do today to achieve your goals? Don't just write them down, mark the most important items and also write down the actions needed. Make all your phone calls at one time, send all your emails one after the other. It's much more efficient to work this way.

By marking down the priority of the most important items and making sure they're completed you avoid the trap of thinking you got a lot accomplished when you've ticked 20 items off your list if they were everyday things like "take dog for walk". Once you've completed the item mark it for follow up on your calendar if you need to.

Never waste a second
I haven't been bored for years. I am always doing something. Whenever my wife asks me to do something I always have to say, ok, I'll be 20 minutes. The reason is I'm always doing something at that precise moment and need to finish it.

I try not to go out and run an "errand" in the car unless I have at least 3 things I need to do. Getting in the car, driving somewhere and back takes time, at least 20 minutes even for something at the end of the road. If you make several of these trips a day you've really eaten into your time. Get similar activities, i.e. things you need to go out to do, done together.

Even "dead time" like standing in line should be used. I'll take a book everywhere with me and read when I can. Large portions of my life have been spent simply waiting for things to happen. I got into the habit of reading just to pass the time and now get through over 100 books a year. "I don't have time to read like you" I hear you say. You go to the bathroom don't you? Put a book in there. 15 minutes reading a day equals 24 books a year, 1,000 books in your lifetime – the equivalent of FIVE college degrees! Over the last few years alone I've read the equivalent of 7 degrees.

You can read while you work out. You can take an audio book while you walk the dog, or drive your car. While you're waiting for your wife to pick out a dress and put her makeup on pick up a magazine and read it. <u>Never waste a second – you can't get it back.</u>

Be solution orientated

Most people look for the problems in life. They look for reasons they can't do things. Some people, like lawyers and bureaucrats are even trained for this. Don't be one of them. If you can't find at least 6 solutions to a problem you're just not trying hard enough. If you can present 6 or more solutions for an issue to a "problem finder" it will show them to be the pain in the ass they really are.

Look for the positives
Every cloud has a silver lining. It sounds trite, but it's true. Every bad thing that happens carries with it a solution that can work better for you. You may not realize it immediately, it may take years to become apparent, but often you can look back and say, "If that didn't happen to me I wouldn't have got this".

I don't have problems, I have opportunities. Now some days are ridden with "opportunity" and I really look forward to a nice cold beer after, but they are opportunities none the less.

Tackle difficult and unpleasant tasks
We all have things we don't want to do. Trying to forget about them doesn't make it any easier, it's usually the reverse. The problem grows and we wind ourselves up worrying about it.

That's why my first call of the day is always the tough one. If there's going to be an argument I'd rather get it over and done with – then I can move on with my life. Let the other guy fume over it all day, it's off my chest now.

Don't procrastinate
It's got to be done sometime, it may as well be now.
You can store time, by the way – when you find yourself with a spare moment, use it to do something you'd have to do later. You may be busy then and wish you'd taken care of it. Clean that stain out of the carpet, cut your fingernails, listen to that language tape. You may not have time to later.
Actions today are money in the bank tomorrow.

Be persistent
Life isn't easy. You may look at someone who's enjoyed "overnight" success on the television, it's rarely that way. Ever watch a swan swimming? It looks so graceful as they

seem to glide across the water. If you were to look underneath you'd see their feet kicking this way and that in an ungainly fashion. It looks easy because you don't see the work involved.

Life is like that. Nothing worthwhile is ever easy. If it's easy everyone would be doing it. You need to keep at it and at it and at it until it's done. No one else is going to achieve your goals for you.

Think for yourself
Just because people tell you things it doesn't mean they're true. It doesn't mean they're right for you, or your situation either. Question what you're told, check out "facts" and develop your own opinions, don't just blindly accept other people's.

Finish your work every day
"Oh I can't do this because I'm too busy". Crap. You're too *lazy* and you don't want to pay the price for success. You've only got to do the work the next day and then you'll be further behind. Make it a habit to clear your desk ever night, you'll be amazed at how much time it saves you in the long run. Think of the number of calls you have to make telling people you'll be late, or you'll get to them "shortly". Just get it done and move on with your life.

If you're really that busy you can't get through your work in 12 hours then just hire someone and delegate the work to them. Stop accepting other people's chores and don't spend time doing things that aren't important or that someone else can't do.

Summary

- ✓ Dress professionally
- ✓ Get a good business card
- ✓ Read what you write before you send it
- ✓ Put agreements in writing
- ✓ Get a contact management program
- ✓ Follow up
- ✓ Get a PDA and keep organized
- ✓ Say no
- ✓ Don't over promise
- ✓ Deliver on your promises
- ✓ Apologize early and often
- ✓ Give realistic quotes
- ✓ Quote in ranges
- ✓ Admit when you're relying on someone else
- ✓ Address your weaknesses
- ✓ Set goals
- ✓ Make to do lists
- ✓ Never waste a second
- ✓ Be solution orientated
- ✓ Look for the positives
- ✓ Tackle difficult and unpleasant tasks
- ✓ Don't procrastinate
- ✓ Be persistent
- ✓ Think for yourself
- ✓ Finish your work every day

Extra *Flake Filter* Forms

We have included these to help you filter out Flakes all on your own. Please fill in these blank forms to apply the lessons you have learned.

Name: ....
Score: ....

Criteria	Score
Have they done an impressive deal before?	
Was it down to them, or others?	
What level do they talk at and what level was their last deal?	
Do they have a track record in what they're doing?	
Do they refer to their business accomplishments, or instead mention previous employers, or education?	
Do they claim expertise they do not possess, or cannot demonstrate?	
How old are they? (Over 40 and unsuccessful is bad)	
Have you made money with them before?	
Has anyone you know made money with them?	
Do they have a financial motivation for dealing with you?	
Is their knowledge accurate?	
Have you caught them out in a lie?	
Do they make a big show of their honesty? ("The lady doth protest too much")	
Do they talk about having the resources to do a deal for 18 months+, but still haven't done it?	
Do they mention numbers in their discussions?	
Do they deliver on their promises?	
Do they return phone calls?	
Have they engineered their own deals, or been in the right place at the right time?	
Do they complete actions on time? Do they say they're "too busy"	
Are you paying them by the hour, a retainer, or are they on a success-based arrangement?	
Do they talk in "MBA speak"?	
Are they often quoted in the press, but never as having done anything?	
Are they punctual?	
Do they like to talk "strategy"?	

Answers

-2	Bad
+2	Good
+1	Not applicable
+1	Lack of information
+10	Shaded box

Scoring

Score	Comment
Ticks in all the shaded boxes, or a score over 30	Solid guy
Score 20-30	OK guy
Score 10-20	Be careful
Score less than 10	Flake

Name: ....
Score: ....

Criteria	Score
Have they done an impressive deal before?	
Was it down to them, or others?	
What level do they talk at and what level was their last deal?	
Do they have a track record in what they're doing?	
Do they refer to their business accomplishments, or instead mention previous employers, or education?	
Do they claim expertise they do not possess, or cannot demonstrate?	
How old are they? (Over 40 and unsuccessful is bad)	
Have you made money with them before?	
Has anyone you know made money with them?	
Do they have a financial motivation for dealing with you?	
Is their knowledge accurate?	
Have you caught them out in a lie?	
Do they make a big show of their honesty? ("The lady doth protest too much")	
Do they talk about having the resources to do a deal for 18 months+, but still haven't done it?	
Do they mention numbers in their discussions?	
Do they deliver on their promises?	
Do they return phone calls?	
Have they engineered their own deals, or been in the right place at the right time?	
Do they complete actions on time? Do they say they're "too busy"	
Are you paying them by the hour, a retainer, or are they on a success-based arrangement?	
Do they talk in "MBA speak"?	
Are they often quoted in the press, but never as having done anything?	
Are they punctual?	
Do they like to talk "strategy"?	

Name: ....
Score: ....

Criteria	Score
Have they done an impressive deal before?	
Was it down to them, or others?	
What level do they talk at and what level was their last deal?	
Do they have a track record in what they're doing?	
Do they refer to their business accomplishments, or instead mention previous employers, or education?	
Do they claim expertise they do not possess, or cannot demonstrate?	
How old are they? (Over 40 and unsuccessful is bad)	
Have you made money with them before?	
Has anyone you know made money with them?	
Do they have a financial motivation for dealing with you?	
Is their knowledge accurate?	
Have you caught them out in a lie?	
Do they make a big show of their honesty? ("The lady doth protest too much")	
Do they talk about having the resources to do a deal for 18 months+, but still haven't done it?	
Do they mention numbers in their discussions?	
Do they deliver on their promises?	
Do they return phone calls?	
Have they engineered their own deals, or been in the right place at the right time?	
Do they complete actions on time? Do they say they're "too busy"	
Are you paying them by the hour, a retainer, or are they on a success-based arrangement?	
Do they talk in "MBA speak"?	
Are they often quoted in the press, but never as having done anything?	
Are they punctual?	
Do they like to talk "strategy"?	

Name: ....
Score: ....

Criteria	Score
Have they done an impressive deal before?	
Was it down to them, or others?	
What level do they talk at and what level was their last deal?	
Do they have a track record in what they're doing?	
Do they refer to their business accomplishments, or instead mention previous employers, or education?	
Do they claim expertise they do not possess, or cannot demonstrate?	
How old are they? (Over 40 and unsuccessful is bad)	
Have you made money with them before?	
Has anyone you know made money with them?	
Do they have a financial motivation for dealing with you?	
Is their knowledge accurate?	
Have you caught them out in a lie?	
Do they make a big show of their honesty? ("The lady doth protest too much")	
Do they talk about having the resources to do a deal for 18 months+, but still haven't done it?	
Do they mention numbers in their discussions?	
Do they deliver on their promises?	
Do they return phone calls?	
Have they engineered their own deals, or been in the right place at the right time?	
Do they complete actions on time? Do they say they're "too busy"	
Are you paying them by the hour, a retainer, or are they on a success-based arrangement?	
Do they talk in "MBA speak"?	
Are they often quoted in the press, but never as having done anything?	
Are they punctual?	
Do they like to talk "strategy"?	

Name: ....

Score: ....

Criteria	Score
Have they done an impressive deal before?	
Was it down to them, or others?	
What level do they talk at and what level was their last deal?	
Do they have a track record in what they're doing?	
Do they refer to their business accomplishments, or instead mention previous employers, or education?	
Do they claim expertise they do not possess, or cannot demonstrate?	
How old are they? (Over 40 and unsuccessful is bad)	
Have you made money with them before?	
Has anyone you know made money with them?	
Do they have a financial motivation for dealing with you?	
Is their knowledge accurate?	
Have you caught them out in a lie?	
Do they make a big show of their honesty? ("The lady doth protest too much")	
Do they talk about having the resources to do a deal for 18 months+, but still haven't done it?	
Do they mention numbers in their discussions?	
Do they deliver on their promises?	
Do they return phone calls?	
Have they engineered their own deals, or been in the right place at the right time?	
Do they complete actions on time? Do they say they're "too busy"	
Are you paying them by the hour, a retainer, or are they on a success-based arrangement?	
Do they talk in "MBA speak"?	
Are they often quoted in the press, but never as having done anything?	
Are they punctual?	
Do they like to talk "strategy"?	

Flake Filter Certificates

Non-Flakiness Appreciation Certificates

If someone has made it through the *Flake Filter* (and you will find out that very few people do), it is only appropriate that you let them know this, and show them how much you appreciate doing business with them. You should fill out one of the certificates on the following pages and give it to them. I understand that this is rather unusual, but if you think someone is not a Flake, then go on, tell them with one of these certificates. This will make you and them feel better if nothing else --and give them something else with which to decorate their office wall space. Besides, you will be part of a national trend toward non-flakiness.

Certificate of Non-Flakiness

Awarded
to:_____

For Non-Flakiness and solidity in general.
You are a pillar of reliability, a beacon in the shadows of mediocrity. You promise, and then you deliver. The world needs more people like you, for you are truly an example to be followed in the business community.
This honor is bestowed upon you by your friend and admirer:

_____

To find our why you are such a superstar and truly valued as a solid citizen, we suggest that you read *The Flake Filter*, available in your nearest bookstore and online. It will show you all your many good qualities, and help you rapidly identify the Flakes of this world that woefully fail to reach your high standards of excellence.

Certificate of Non-Flakiness

Awarded to: _____

For Non-Flakiness and solidity in general.

You are a pillar of reliability, a beacon in the shadows of mediocrity. You promise, and then you deliver. The world needs more people like you, for you are truly an example to be followed in the business community.

This honor is bestowed upon you by your friend and admirer:

To find our why you are such a superstar and truly valued as a solid citizen, we suggest that you read *The Flake Filter*, available in your nearest bookstore and online. It will show you all your many good qualities, and help you rapidly identify the Flakes of this world that woefully fail to reach your high standards of excellence.

Certificate of Non-Flakiness

Awarded
to:_____

For Non-Flakiness and solidity in general.

You are a pillar of reliability, a beacon in the shadows of mediocrity. You promise, and then you deliver. The world needs more people like you, for you are truly an example to be followed in the business community.

This honor is bestowed upon you by your friend and admirer:

_____

To find our why you are such a superstar and truly valued as a solid citizen, we suggest that you read *The Flake Filter*, available in your nearest bookstore and online. It will show you all your many good qualities, and help you rapidly identify the Flakes of this world that woefully fail to reach your high standards of excellence.

Certificate of Non-Flakiness

Awarded
to:_____

For Non-Flakiness and solidity in general.
You are a pillar of reliability, a beacon in the shadows of mediocrity. You promise, and then you deliver. The world needs more people like you, for you are truly an example to be followed in the business community.
This honor is bestowed upon you by your friend and admirer:

To find our why you are such a superstar and truly valued as a solid citizen, we suggest that you read *The Flake Filter*, available in your nearest bookstore and online. It will show you all your many good qualities, and help you rapidly identify the Flakes of this world that woefully fail to reach your high standards of excellence.

Certificate of Non-Flakiness

Awarded
to:_____

For Non-Flakiness and solidity in general.
You are a pillar of reliability, a beacon in the shadows of mediocrity. You promise, and then you deliver. The world needs more people like you, for you are truly an example to be followed in the business community.
This honor is bestowed upon you by your friend and admirer:

_____

To find our why you are such a superstar and truly valued as a solid citizen, we suggest that you read *The Flake Filter*, available in your nearest bookstore and online. It will show you all your many good qualities, and help you rapidly identify the Flakes of this world that woefully fail to reach your high standards of excellence.

Certificate of Flakiness

If someone has drastically failed the *Flake Filter* and wasted your time, you ought to let them know that too. Obviously, this judgment it entirely down to you, but you can always fill in one of the certificates below and fax it to them anonymously at their office. Who knows, you might shame them into changing their horrible ways. We can only hope.

Fax Message

Fax to: _____

Pages: 1 of 1

Certificate of Flakiness

Awarded
to:_____

For being a total, utter Flake and wasting people's time. You are a total Flake. You make promises you cannot keep. You could not organize a night of drunken debauchery in a brewery. You are a total waste of time and space. We suggest that you go and get a job in government, as you clearly have no right to be attempting to deal in the business world.
This shame is bestowed upon you with much regret.

To find our why someone thinks you are such a Flake and to attempt to mend your ways, we suggest that you read *the Flake Filter*, available at your nearest bookstore or online. It will show you all your many faults, how to spot others like you, and more importantly, how to identify solid, decent business people to try to emulate.

Fax Message

Fax to: _____

Pages: 1 of 1

Certificate of Flakiness

Awarded

to: _____

For being a total, utter Flake and wasting people's time.
You are a total Flake. You make promises you cannot keep. You could not organize a night of drunken debauchery in a brewery. You are a total waste of time and space. We suggest that you go and get a job in government, as you clearly have no right to be attempting to deal in the business world.
This shame is bestowed upon you with much regret.

To find our why someone thinks you are such a Flake and to attempt to mend your ways, we suggest that you read *the Flake Filter*, available at your nearest bookstore or online. It will show you all your many faults, how to spot others like you, and more importantly, how to identify solid, decent business people to try to emulate.

Fax Message

Fax to: _____

Pages: 1 of 1

Certificate of Flakiness
Awarded
to: _____

For being a total, utter Flake and wasting people's time.
You are a total Flake. You make promises you cannot keep. You could not organize a night of drunken debauchery in a brewery. You are a total waste of time and space. We suggest that you go and get a job in government, as you clearly have no right to be attempting to deal in the business world.
  This shame is bestowed upon you with much regret.

To find our why someone thinks you are such a Flake and to attempt to mend your ways, we suggest that you read *the Flake Filter*, available at your nearest bookstore or online. It will show you all your many faults, how to spot others like you, and more importantly, how to identify solid, decent business people to try to emulate.

Fax Message

Fax to: _____

Pages: 1 of 1

Certificate of Flakiness

Awarded
to:_____
For being a total, utter Flake and wasting people's time.

You are a total Flake. You make promises you cannot keep. You could not organize a night of drunken debauchery in a brewery. You are a total waste of time and space. We suggest that you go and get a job in government, as you clearly have no right to be attempting to deal in the business world.
This shame is bestowed upon you with much regret.

To find our why someone thinks you are such a Flake and to attempt to mend your ways, we suggest that you read *the Flake Filter*, availabe at your nearest bookstore or online. It will show you all your many faults, how to spot others like you, and more importantly, how to identify solid, decent business people to try to emulate.

Fax Message

Fax to: _____

Pages: 1 of 1

Certificate of Flakiness

Awarded

to:_____

For being a total, utter Flake and wasting people's time.

You are a total Flake. You make promises you cannot keep. You could not organize a night of drunken debauchery in a brewery. You are a total waste of time and space. We suggest that you go and get a job in government, as you clearly have no right to be attempting to deal in the business world.

This shame is bestowed upon you with much regret.

To find our why someone thinks you are such a Flake and to attempt to mend your ways, we suggest that you read *the Flake Filter*, available at your nearest bookstore or online. It will show you all your many faults, how to spot others like you, and more importantly, how to identify solid, decent business people to try to emulate.

Your Opinions

Earlier, I promised you space all your own, where you could write down your own opinions. Please do not send them to me, because I really don't care. I do, however, keep my word. The following space is just for you, and it is all your own. Please take this time to "get it out of your system." Whatever is burning you up, please write it down for your own benefit(s). Enjoy.

Acknowledgements (again)

O.K., now that you have come this far, we will now tell you that these are the people that have helped me out. For the most part, they are pretty good and solid people. Any errors, omissions and other things that I messed up are solely down to me:

- I could not have got to this stage without the help of Chris Hurn, he helped arrange the original *Flake Filter* into a professional version we could do something with.
- Earl Ratliff, Andrew Stewart, Dr Roger Murray, Jim Bourgeois and James Sheridan for all their proof reading help.
- Dr James "Doc" Eisenbud – The young man knows the rules, but the old man knows the exceptions.
- Robbie Van Roijen.
- Lastly Allen D'Angelo who led me past the, very many, flaky people in the publishing business.

About the Author

Toby Unwin
After running and selling one of the most profitable Internet businesses in Europe he retired, aged 26, worth(on paper) over $160M.

He married a former model and Ivy League graduate then retired to, what he calls, "*The Promised Land*". (He spent 3 years living out his James Bond fantasies). He is an accomplished pilot, who holds every fixed wing rating and reads over 100 books a year.

Now he's back, and this time it's personal. In addition to writing *The Flake Filter* he also co-authored the Best Selling, *Practice Without Fear*.

He is regularly consulted by businesses, high net worth individuals and is Internet Strategy consultant to a United Nations Affiliate.

He can be contacted at:
101374.1407@compuserve.com

How can I help you?

You know now how much time not dealing with flakes can save you, but what about your company, your co-workers and the people you do business with?

Book quantity discounts and branding
The most precious gift you can give someone is time. Forget about executive pen sets and branded golf balls. These things get lost, and your message along with them. If you give someone this book they'll read it. They'll also see your branding and any promotional material you want to add inside. People don't throw books away, so your message will stay with them for years to come.

Seminars
- Want to get together with some likeminded people you can really do business with?
- Would you like to find out how you can really make these principles work for you?
- Do you want to take being a successful individual to the next level and really achieve something with your life?

Then you need to come to a *Flake Filter* seminar.

Training
- How much time do your salespeople spend chasing the wrong prospects, people who ultimately end up letting them down and not placing an order?
- Would you like to be able to rely on your staff to get the job done?

I can start to fix your problems today.

Consulting
- How many hiring decisions have you regretted? They came from a good company, went to the right school, but ultimately couldn't be relied upon to get the job done. Wouldn't it be nice if your Human Resources department could figure this out *before* you go to the expense of hiring someone?
- Are your staff's incentives in line with your corporate goals?
- How much more profitable would your company be if your people didn't spend time "spinning their wheels" chasing unreliable people?

You need our help - Pay us by the result, not the hour.

If you don't take action no one else will do it for you.

You can contact me at:
101374.1407@compuserve.com

NOTES

Printed in the United States
1231400001B/361-588